WHAT'S RIGHT
ABOUT AMERICA

CELEBRATING OUR NATION'S VALUES

REP. KAY GRANGER

World Ahead Publishing, Inc.

Published by World Ahead Publishing, Inc., Los Angeles, CA

World Ahead Publishing's books are available at special discounts for bulk purchases. World Ahead Publishing also publishes books in electronic formats. For more information, visit www.worldahead.com.

First Edition

ISBN 0-9778984-0-7
LCCN 2006926795

Printed in the United States of America

10 9 8 7 6 5 4 3 2 1

To J.D., Martha, Brandon, Logan, and Jack

CONTENTS

SECTION ONE: LIFE

SECTION TWO: LIBERTY

SECTION THREE:
THE PURSUIT OF HAPPINESS

FOREWORD

A S A FORMER TEACHER, mother and politician, Congress-woman Kay Granger's perspective on American history and the importance of the country's values is unique and inspiring. *What's Right About America* struck a chord with me on a professional and personal level. Granger uses American stories to demonstrate how and why American values such as freedom, equality, justice and compassion are universal. As a philanthropist and deep believer in the power of values, I found her arguments compelling and provocative. As a mother, I was moved by Congresswoman Granger's urgent battle cry to teach children about American values—first, as a matter of inheritance and second, to secure America's freedom and safety in years to come. *What's Right About America* is at once a great read and a bible for anyone interested in the past, present and future of the American value system.

Sarah Ferguson
Duchess of York

PREFACE

AS I WRITE THESE WORDS, America is at war. The vision that the terrorists offer the world is one that demands a response. Not just a military one, which our troops are handling in fine fashion. And not just an economic one, which continues to roar because of the American economic engine. But more importantly, the vision of the terrorists must be confronted with ideas, with values, with principles. We are beating the terrorists on the battlefields of Afghanistan and Iraq. But are we beating them on the battlefield of ideas? Much has been said about the battle for the hearts and minds of the Arab world. But there is another struggle going on as well. And that's the struggle for the hearts and minds of America's children. There are many gifts we hand down to our young ones. But shouldn't we also make sure that as part of their inheritance we teach them about one of the greatest gifts of all, the gift of being free and being an American?

As we teach others about freedom, perhaps we could do a better job of teaching our own. The story of the heroism of September 11, 2001, reminds us of the greatness of our past and points us to the promise of our future. For there is much we can be proud of in the actions of those Americans who fought back on September 11, and even more we can learn. They weren't just fighting. They were fighting for something bigger than themselves. And they fought and died in noble and heroic ways. In their courage we can find our challenge—to know what it means to be an American and how to fight for it.

Where do we start? How can we renew our commitment to our enduring principles? How can we ensure that future generations of Americans are able and willing to fight for the gift of freedom given to us by God and written into law by our Founding Fathers? As a former teacher, I have seen how impressionable young minds can be. I know that the America of tomorrow is being molded in the classrooms of today. And I know that teachers are our first line of defense in ensuring that America's children know about their country's greatness. Teachers are special. As I often say, most people spend their lives building careers, but teachers spend their careers building lives. Every day they sow the seeds that will one day grow into a nation's future. So when it comes to our children, it is vitally important that we teach things right, and that we teach the right things. The same is true for parents. The power of your leadership stretches deep into the future. What you teach your kids today they will put into practice tomorrow.

What is it that we should teach our children? How to read and how to write? Yes. How to add and how to subtract? Absolutely. And what about helping young people gain a good grasp of the scientific world and the technology revolution? Now more than ever. The good news is that many teachers all across the country are doing a great job of making sure our children are making the grade on most of these topics. The bad news is that other subjects in education are not being taught. It's not the fault of the teachers. Or of the parents. Or even school boards and administrators. Instead, it's the result of a trend. The past forty years have seen politics and political correctness dictate to teachers that they are to stay away from one of the most important subjects in education. As a result, our students are paying the price.

What is it that we have forgotten to include in the education of our young people? We often hear that there is no prayer in school. What is even truer is that there is little Americanism in school. Students no longer learn American values because we no longer teach them. A story is told that as the Constitutional Convention was ending in 1787, a Philadelphia woman approached Benjamin Franklin and asked him what the men at the convention had given the nation. "A republic," Franklin responded, "if you can keep it."

More than two hundred years later, the challenge remains. We are still the United States of America. We remain the freest place on earth. But can we keep it? How do we keep it? We keep it by passing onto the next generation a sense of what was and what is to come; a belief in the greatness of our past and in the glory of our future. We can only do this if we teach our kids what it means to be an American. This book is an effort to help do just that. Its structure is simple, but its message is profound. The book is organized around the same principles that define the Declaration of Independence. In making the case to the world, Thomas Jefferson spoke of the natural rights that every American owns and that every human is entitled to claim as his own—life, liberty, and the pursuit of happiness. If the Declaration of Independence is our national birth certificate, then these principles are our birthright. Our nation was born out of a struggle to protect and secure these rights, and in many ways that battle continues to this day. In a very real sense, the American Revolution never really ended. It continues every time any American anywhere claims these rights as his own and uses them to make a better world.

There are three sections of the book: one each on life, liberty, and the pursuit of happiness—the pillars that make up our democracy. But beyond the pillars of every beautiful home, many different rooms exist inside that make the house complete. Similarly, there are many other values that make our three natural rights whole. For example, what does it mean to be a nation that values life? Or that values liberty? Or the pursuit of happiness? In each section of the book, we will look at several applications of these three great principles and what they mean to us as Americans. Each chapter will tell stories demonstrating why this theme is important. Each chapter will not only discuss why it is important to teach these values to students but how to teach them. At the end of the book, there is a list of important primary documents in our history, as well as a guide to promote thought and discussion. Being born an American is only part of what makes you an American. It also has to be learned—which is to say, it has to be taught.

You, as a teacher or a parent, are on the front lines in the struggle to equip a new generation of Americans with the intellectual tools they will need to keep us free and safe. It is a battle you cannot avoid and you must not lose. Our nation—and our future—depend on it.

ACKNOWLEDGEMENTS

I HAVE BEEN BLESSED with help and inspiration all along the way with this book. In the spring of 1996 I had the good fortune to meet a remarkable young man named Kasey S. Pipes. He joined my staff and has remained my friend and confidant for ten years. I thank him for his support on this project. I have also had the privilege of working closely over the years with Ken Mehlman. His support was also greatly appreciated. Over the years, so many talented staffers have helped form the Granger team, including Barrett Benge Karr, Johnnie Kaberle, Darin Gardner, Violet Love and Dodie Souder. And the team I have today is outstanding: Barbara Ragland, Robert Head, Amy Tenhouse, Stacey Kounelias, Caitlin Carroll, Rachel Carter, Catherine Knowles, Jane Edson, Andrew Acker, Melody Parlett, Pat Svacina, Sally Burt, Marcia Etie, Danielle Gonzalez, Bonnie O'Leary, Kelsey Marquez, Paul Nenninger, Michael Gonzales and Terry Edwards.

As I wrote to inspire parents and teachers about our American story and our American values, my mother Alliene Mullendore was never out of my thoughts. She inspired me as she did my sister, Lynn O'Day, and my three children: Chelsea Hughes, Brandon Granger and J.D. Granger. I was encouraged in this endeavor by H. Lee Graham who is the real writer in the family.

Those who listened to my experiences and wrestled with the meaning of September 11 back home are always an encouragement to me. Mary Palko, Tim and Elaine Petrus, Barbara Ferrell, Becky Haskin, Alice and Foy Holland, Lynn Manny, Sarah Saylor, David and Ann Chappell, Marty Leonard, Judy Needham, Louise and Gordon England, Dionne Bagsby, Norma Roby, Rosa Navejar, Mark Hill, Bill Meadows, Ted Blevins, James

Toal, Lt. Col. Tom Hayden (Ret.), and Dee Kelly are just a few upon whose friendship I depend.

I have also had the opportunity to serve with people whose service to their community, state and nation are inspirational to me. These include Bob Bolen, Gordon England, Mike Moncrief and Pete Geren. My friends in the Congress are many, but during and after September 11 the friendship of Roy Blunt, Dennis Hastert, Sue Myrick, Kevin Brady, Mac Thornberry, Sam Johnson, Dave Camp and Henry Bonilla were important as we sought answers to the why of this terrible event.

There are those who hold me in their prayers and sustain me, including Pastor Bob Nichols, Charles Prior, Larry Ragland and Dr. Wayne Day. Those who serve our students at every level are my heroes. My conversations over the years with educators have kept me focused on educating our young people. They include Dr. Jennifer Brooks, Dr. Leonardo de la Garza, Dr. Judith Carrier and Dr. Jake Schrum.

Finally I would like to thank Elliot Goldman and the entire World Ahead team for making the dream of this book a reality. Eric Jackson, Ami Naramor and Judy Abarbanel all did great work in moving this book from my computer to your bookstore.

INTRODUCTION

"And what the dead had no speech for, when living,
They can tell you, being dead; the communication
Of the dead is tongued with fire beyond the language of the living."

—T.S. Eliot, 1942

THE FIRST MOMENTS of dawn reveal a broad green expanse of swaying trees, and rolling hills gently guard an open space that is now among the most hallowed places in America. Flowers can usually be seen. Crying can sometimes be heard. And pride can always be felt by those who enter. Many come to pay honor to this place. It was here, on this field in Somerset County, Pennsylvania, that forty people transcended mortality. They left earth to touch the face of God. But their touch can still be felt on earth. They are gone but not forgotten, dead but still living. Their story and their words still call out to us. For their sacrifice was not an end, but a beginning. Indeed, a permanent memorial is under construction that will forever enshrine the heroism of that day.

Early on the morning of September 11, 2001, forty passengers boarded a plane in Newark, New Jersey and entered history. They were a normal group of people who unknowingly had a date with destiny. Yet in their own unique way, each was perfectly prepared for what lay ahead.

Jason Dahl was a pilot who had learned to fly a plane before he could drive a car. He loved his career. But he loved his wife more. He volunteered to fly United Airlines Flight 93 so that he could be home in time to celebrate his wedding anniversary with his wife.

Debbie Welsh was the perfect flight attendant. She was a caring sort, the kind of person who would take unused airplane meals home with her to share with the less fortunate in her New York neighborhood. Not surprisingly, her colleagues called her the "Little Apostle of the Airlines."

Nicole Miller was a college student. She was on her way back from seeing her boyfriend in New York. Everyone who ever met her was enchanted by her charisma and gentle spirit. The salesman who sold her a cell phone would later call Nicole's parents to say he had only been with her a few minutes, but he was amazed at her innate sweetness.

Todd Beamer was a successful businessman on yet another business trip. In the busyness of living, he never lost sight of the business of life. He had a deep and abiding faith. And he couldn't wait to board the redeye flight the next day to return to his wife and kids.

There were others. Business owners. Blue-collar workers. Writers. Teachers. Even a bartender. Every person was unique. Yet every one was the same. They were all human beings; good and decent people trying to get to their destination to do a job. But they were all destined for immortality. Each one would play an important role in the opening battle of a worldwide war.

They were forty heroes that day, but they were really one. For on that fateful September morning, all of them were united in one spirit, one cause, one fateful moment in history. As the plane took off from Newark, it banked to the west and began the journey to San Francisco. The passengers settled down for a long flight. Some began to catch up on sleep; others sought to catch up on work. And they were all expecting a peaceful, uneventful flight.

But the forty heroes were not alone on the plane. Four others joined them that day. They were unlike the forty Americans. Theirs was a mission of death. The night before, they received instructions for their mission encouraging them to be brave during the slaughter that was to come. Not long after the flight took off, the terrorists took over. They stood up and placed red bandanas on their heads. Then they forced their way into the cockpit. An accented voice announced over the intercom that a bomb was on board. The plane would have to go back.

Up to then, what had happened was frightening, but not unique. For years terrorists have hijacked planes and issued demands. But it was at this exact moment that the story of Flight 93 became historic. This was the moment when something so unusual happened that the terrorists were caught off guard. The four hijackers made their plans. But they didn't plan on one thing—the response of the forty Americans. The ordinary people of Flight 93 were about to do something extraordinary.

They decided to fight back.

The passengers quietly and quickly assembled in the back of the plane. In the next few moments they would conduct themselves in a way that was very determined, very courageous, and, above all, very American.

Much has been said and written about the Flight 93 passengers taking down their plane. Less has been said and written about how they went about it. It wasn't impulse. It wasn't fear. And it wasn't spontaneous. It was a careful, deliberate, and well-planned response in the first battle of the War on Terror.

What did the passengers do? First, they held a meeting. Like their forefathers in Philadelphia, these passengers met to discuss a grave crisis and what should be done about it. Then they voted. In a scene that has been repeated throughout the story of America, ordinary citizens met and discussed a variety of options. You can just imagine them debating what to do with their lives on the line. How amazing it is to think that in the middle of this storm of danger, these passengers had the presence of mind to come together and vote on a plan of action. Very amazing, indeed. And very American.

Having met together and voted, the passengers moved forward with their plan. They spoke with the eloquence of their actions. They were not afraid, and they were not to be denied. They met the terrorists on the battlefield chosen by the enemy and scored a triumph for freedom. They took the plane down.

The passengers of Flight 93 were not victims; they were victors. Their plan worked and their selfless actions saved countless lives down below. Throughout the years and throughout the world, people have sought to define America. Poets with poems, musicians with songs, and writers with prose have all searched for the key to unlock the mystery of America. But the most eloquent words and the most beautiful music can never say as much about America as the quiet courage of the passengers of Flight 93.

What is it that compels forty strangers to bond together and give their lives so that they might save the lives of others? Where do ordinary people get the extraordinary courage to confront evil and prevail? And why would these people feel it was necessary to fight back? America is a place unlike any other on earth. Most countries are defined as a nation that has a people. But here in America, we are a people who happen to make up a nation. Here the people come first. Here the people rule. We are a people defined not by where we live but by what we believe. We are unique not only because of our culture and our history, but, more important, because of our freedoms.

It is precisely because of our freedoms that terrorists have declared war. Many things can be said about the terrorists of September 11. One thing we can't say is that they didn't know what they were doing. They knew exactly what they were doing and exactly why they were doing it.

They did it because they hated us. They hated our freedom. They hated our principles. They hated the very idea of a nation where "all men are created equal" and every person can pursue happiness in his own way. It is well documented that the terrorists chose their September 11 targets carefully, and they chose them wisely. The targets they selected sent a message about why they were declaring war on us. Not only could they kill thousands of people at work in New York, they could take down a grand symbol of American enterprise and economic power. Not only could they kill military officials at the Pentagon, they could strike a blow against the most famous military installation in the world.

But not only did the terrorists know why they hated us, they knew what they were fighting for. They wanted to spread their evil gospel across the globe. Theirs was a dark, menacing philosophy that would put women in their place and put non-Muslims in danger of losing their lives. A world ruled by the September 11 terrorists would be a place where freedom is replaced by fear and justice is replaced by tyranny. There would be no rights, no civil liberties, no peace, no rule of law. This is no way to run the world, but it is precisely the world the terrorists had in mind.

This book is about a different way, a different world where people who are free and equal have responsibilities and rights, based upon the God-given gifts of life, liberty, and the pursuit of happiness. This book is about America; and the values that make this country great. It seeks to explain why these values are important in our history and essential to our future. I hope you enjoy reading it as much as I've enjoyed writing it. This is your country and these are your values. Embrace them, defend them, and above all, be proud of them.

SECTION ONE

LIFE

CHAPTER ONE

WE VALUE
THE INDIVIDUAL

"This is Basher-52. I'm alive!"

—Captain Scott O'Grady, 1995

FOR THE UNITED STATES and its NATO allies, June 2, 1995, was another day in the struggle to bring peace and justice to Bosnia. But for Captain Scott O'Grady, this was to be the first day in the most trying week of his life. The clear blue skies masked the dark storm clouds of personal challenge that would soon confront the twenty-nine-year-old. Like so many other military officers, O'Grady was young, talented, and confident. He was an asset to the Air Force and a credit to his country. A graduate of the prestigious Embry-Riddle Aeronautical University, O'Grady always wanted to fly. After receiving his commission, he donned his Air Force wings with pride. His dream had always been to fly F-16s. That's exactly what he did. He knew how to handle a plane, and he knew how to complete his mission. On this early June day, he was about to set out on his forty-seventh—and most memorable—mission since the fighting began.

His call sign for the mission was "Basher-52." On that June morning he flew five miles up into the sky over the Bosnian countryside. It was eerie how peaceful things could seem from the cockpit of a fighter jet designed for combat. His plane was surrounded by pale blue skies above him and green countryside below him. It was all so beautiful. Yet so dangerous. Enemy patrols lurked below, searching for any NATO plane to attack. Armed with surface-to-air missiles, they waited. And waited. And waited. And then...

The first salvo missed O'Grady's F-16. Barely. The second one didn't. O'Grady, realizing what had happened, relied on all his instincts and training. He calmly exited the plane and parachuted to the ground. He was safe from the plane but not from danger. It must have been terrifying to know that he would soon be landing in enemy territory. The same people who shot down his plane would soon search for O'Grady to finish the job. For the next six days, O'Grady hid himself among the brush and bushes of the countryside. He came out only at night and survived on grass and ants. Still, there was no sign of a rescue mission and little hope of making it out alive.

Then on the sixth night, Captain Thomas "T.O." Hanford, an F-16 pilot from O'Grady's own squadron, picked up a faint signal. A radio exchange ensued between the two:

"This is Basher Five Two...I'm alive!" O'Grady cried into the frequency, hoping for a response.

"Basher Five Two, what was your squadron in Korea?" came the reply from Hanford, who could hardly believe his ears and wanted to confirm O'Grady's identify.

"Juvats! Juvats!" O'Grady responded.

"Copy that, you're alive!" yelled Hanford. "Good to hear your voice."

The rescue began.

Just a few moments after this exchange, Captain Hanford relayed the information to his commanders. An AWACS plane identified the location of O'Grady's frequency. Within hours, forty planes and helicopters were on their way. Two Super Stallion helicopters from the 24th Marine Expeditionary Unit landed within fifty yards of O'Grady's hiding place. Two minutes after that, O'Grady was safely on board and the helicopters were off the ground.

The story of the rescue of O'Grady is well known by many Americans. What is not as well known is how unique this story is. This ordinary tale of American heroism would be unthinkable in much of the world. Military strategy is based on marshalling one's resources and attacking the enemy's center of gravity. Casualties and prisoners are simply a part of war that must be accepted. Yet in America, home of the greatest military the world has ever seen, a slightly different philosophy can be seen in the story of O'Grady.

We believe that every individual is precious, and every life is worth saving.

Stop and think about the rescue of O'Grady. Think of the extraordinary use of technology—from the F-16 to the AWACs plane to the forty aircraft used in the rescue. Consider the astonishing precision and intelligence which led the Marines to find and extract O'Grady. Think of the planning and preparation that went into making this rescue work with the finest military technology and leadership in the world. Hardware, costing billions of dollars, were invested in this operation. And it was an operation to save exactly one person.

How many other nations would do this? How many would risk lives and equipment to save one pilot? And why are we so willing to save one American?

Americans love life. Every life. We value the young and the old. We cherish those who are healthy and those with disabilities. Just look around you. You will see the monuments of this nation to its people. All of its people. Down the street you will see the public school where the tax dollars of citizens are spent to educate the young. In your grandparents' mailboxes they receive Social Security checks and assistance for health care through Medicare and Medicaid. Go into any building and you will notice ramps next to the stairs. This is required by law to give Americans with disabilities equal access. In fact, in true American fashion, that is the name of the law: the Americans with Disabilities Act.

All of these are examples of America's commitment to every individual life. We believe in the sanctity of life at all stages, at all times. So it should surprise no one that our military is the finest in the world and will use its manpower and resources to help find and save one single soldier. But it might surprise a lot of folks that we are virtually the only country that does this. In most nations, the loss of a single soldier is the inevitable cost of battle. To Americans, it is a new challenge that must be met with a battle plan.

Stop and think about how unique this is. Compare how America values life with other parts of the world.

Do you know slavery still exists in some parts of the world such as India and Brazil? Do you know about the rampant sex trafficking of little girls in Albania? Or about the sweat labor shops in El Salvador where young children give everything they have for almost nothing in exchange? Or about the one-child policy in China? Or about women having second-class status in Ethiopia, Mexico, and Kuwait?

These are all problems that are still experienced in the 21st century in our world. But not here. Not in America. Here life is more precious. While Americans certainly have our faults, we generally get it right. Just look at some of our more recent history. America liberated the Jews from the Holocaust and the concentration camps. We set free the people of Japan from their oppressive, fascist rulers. We fought to protect the sovereignty and the lives of the people of South Korea and South Vietnam. Today, in Afghanistan and Iraq we are helping to build free governments so the lives of the people—all the people—are respected and protected.

Closer to home, we have not always been faithful to our mission of honoring life. But we usually get it right in the end. The story of America contains heroic chapters by Americans who fought for voting rights for women, an end to child labor, and equal pay for all.

Perhaps most famously, we struggled to have the courage of our convictions and enact civil rights laws to protect all Americans. For too long, blacks and other minorities were denied the same basic rights as other Americans. One of the most fascinating aspects of Dr. Martin Luther King Jr.'s strategy was draping his quest for civil rights in the fabric of America's founding. He rightly claimed that the Founding Fathers had "signed a promissory note to which every American was to fall heir." It has taken us some time. But in the end, America has eventually honored its commitment to protect the rights of "life, liberty, and the pursuit of happiness" for all Americans.

In doing so, we are keeping the faith with our founding and our forefathers. Thomas Jefferson wrote that the only legitimate object of a government was the "care of human life and happiness." King called it the "promise of democracy."

May it ever be so.

CHAPTER TWO

WE VALUE
THE FAMILY

*"I am quite content to go now and to leave
my children at least an honorable name."*

—Theodore Roosevelt, 1898

ONE HUNDRED YEARS AGO, few stars shone as bright in
the American constellation as Theodore Roosevelt's. As a
soldier and statesman, Roosevelt embraced and embodied
American values in a way few other Americans ever have. As
he once said, "In any moment of decision, the best thing you
can do is the right thing. The worst thing you can do is nothing." A man of action, of vision, and above all, of courage, Roosevelt's steely resolve held him in good stead during the fires of
life's challenges. Here was a man who, one afternoon in Cuba,
put his convictions into action in an event that he later described as "the great day of my life."

It was during the Spanish-American War that Roosevelt
achieved his moment of martial glory. On the morning of July 1,
1898, Roosevelt, then a colonel in the Army, led a group of soldiers that would forever be known as the Rough Riders. These
men began the day near the San Juan Heights, a series of hills,
where Roosevelt would make history. This would be the scene
of one of the most famous charges in American history. Roosevelt's greatest and longest day began with preparing his men.
Then he and his men waited. They waited while artillery gun-

ners opened the battle. They waited for their chance to make a mark in the battle and in the history of their country.

After moving his troops into position, Roosevelt decided to act. He asked for permission to advance. He proposed to take a key position known as Kettle Hill. To his delight, the request was given, and he was ready to get moving. "The instant I received the order," he later wrote, "I sprang on my horse, and then my 'crowded hour' began."

On top of a horse named Texas, Roosevelt, a natural leader who always led by example, was in his element and in command. This day would be no different. He was utterly unafraid as he led his men forward and up the hill. "Are you afraid to stand up when I am on horseback?" he asked soldiers who were afraid. How could they not follow his leadership? How could they not follow his example?

As shells exploded and men began to fall, Roosevelt and his troops continued forward. The steel of the Spanish bullets was strong, but not as strong as Roosevelt's soul. He was fearless, moving forward, leading his men. At one point, the Rough Riders came upon some American soldiers whose advance had been thwarted by the Spanish. But Roosevelt would not be stopped. Not by the Spanish. Not even by Americans. He gave the order for the stalled unit to move forward. When they wouldn't move forward, he moved them aside: "Then let my men through!" Roosevelt and his men had a date with destiny. Nothing could hold them back.

On he went. As he continued up the hill, he taunted death by waving his white hat in the air. He was invincible and unintimidated. When his horse was held up by a fence, he carried on by foot. When a bullet grazed his elbow, he shook it off. When Roosevelt at last reached the summit of Kettle Hill, he was the first one there. As his troops soon joined him and took command of the hill, Roosevelt looked out over the horizon and saw another battle raging. Only seven hundred yards away, American troops were fighting their way up San Juan Hill. To Roosevelt, it appeared that the Spanish were holding off the Americans. "Obviously," he said, "the proper thing to do was help them."

He began this second assault by ordering a continuous volley-fire for ten minutes. Then, having softened the Spanish lines, he charged forward. Down Kettle Hill his men went and up San Juan Hill. The air soon filled with the sounds of gunfire, but Roosevelt was once again unafraid. His men surged forward until they reached the top of the hill. When the Spanish soldiers spotted the onslaught of the Rough Riders, they ran for their lives. San Juan Hill was secured. And so was Theodore Roosevelt's place in history.

<>

That night, as Roosevelt surveyed the remains on the battlefield, his first thought was not of his own heroics or even those of his men. His first thought was of his family. "Should the worst come to the worst," he told a friend, "I am quite content to go now and to leave my children at least an honorable name."

How striking that for Roosevelt, the Battle of San Juan Hill was about more than personal heroism or national security, but rather about his relationship to his family. He told another friend that the battle was his "one chance to cut my little notch in the stick that stands as a measuring rod in every family."

San Juan Hill may have been his greatest triumph but family was his greatest love.

It is not an overstatement to say that Roosevelt was one of the first to practice the politics of family values, but he also valued families. Sometimes his devotion to family was over the top, as when he urged American men and women to have as many babies as possible in order to sufficiently populate America. But some of his words ring true even today. For example, he argued that healthy families make for a healthy nation. He said families are the basis of our country. Roosevelt believed what the famous observer of all things American, Alexis de Tocqueville once wrote: "Where family pride ceases to act, individual selfishness comes into play."

Before America was founded, some believed that a strong government, preferably a monarchy, was needed to keep people at peace with themselves. Some feared that a republic would give individuals too much freedom leading to anarchy. The Founding Fathers knew that a vibrant republic required a virtuous people, and the family is one of the ways we create people of virtue. Children depend on their families to raise them and teach them, to correct them and love them. Great Americans have always understood that they were created by their families.

Abraham Lincoln once said, "All I am, or can be, I owe to my angel mother." Most of us can say the same thing. Our parents helped make us who we are and helped show us where to go. Families give us a sense of roots and a pair of wings. First, they bestow upon us a sense of where we have come from and what we believe in. My mother worked hard as a teacher and a mother. From her, I learned that nothing worthwhile is ever easy, and that success in life is usually a product of how hard you work. My mother also helped instill in me a sense of concern for the community and a sense of compassion for those around me. The family is where we first learn our values.

Second, family gives us a pair of wings. They encourage us to set goals and achieve them. After watching my mother all those years, I knew I could reach my goals. That's what family does—it gives you a belief in you. I know that many children today don't have two parents; others have painful relationships with their parents. That's okay. There are other people who can help: a friend or a grandparent or a neighbor.

The key is to remember that even if you haven't had the best family situation, family is still an important American value. Someday, you may get married and have your own family. Work hard at it. If you become a parent someday, remember that raising your kids is your most important job. Nothing more, nothing less.

Teach your children. Make time for them. Go to their Little League games. Check their homework. Even if your parents didn't do these things for you, do it for your kids. Give them the love that you deserved and that they need. Like Roosevelt, at all times, in all things, conduct yourself in a way that will make your family proud. Your children will watch you. What will they see?

Above all, don't just talk about family values, actually value families.

CHAPTER THREE

WE VALUE
THE COMMUNITY

"When you are good to others, you are best to yourself."

—Benjamin Franklin

THIS IS THE STORY of perhaps George Washington's greatest and least-known victory. A battle won not with weapons, but words. And it might have been the battle that saved America.

The men were tired, broke, and angry. After years of fighting the British and the Hessians, the American army was still looking for a fight. History is filled with the stories of victorious armies turning on themselves, and that was about to happen in Newburgh, New York in March, 1783.

Two years after conquering British General Charles Cornwallis at Yorktown, Virginia, American troops remained in the field awaiting the results of the Paris Peace Treaty. British rule was coming to an end. That much was certain. But who would rule once they left? And what kind of government would Americans forge for themselves?

Perhaps these questions were on the minds of the American troops as they gathered in Newburgh that spring. History records that at least one important issue was very much on the minds of the men—money. While men like Benjamin Franklin, John Jay, and John Adams were in Paris seeking peace, men like General Horatio Gates were in Newburgh stirring up trouble.

Gates had a valid case—Congress had no money. Congress was unable to even pay the interests on its loans, much less the salaries of its soldiers. And yet if anyone deserved to be paid, it was the soldiers. They alone had known the hardships of Valley Forge. They alone had faced down the British at Princeton, New Jersey and Yorktown. And they alone had won the freedom of America on the battlefields of war.

The seeds of discontent were already deeply planted when Gates and others began seeking a harvest of rage. History is etched with attempted mutinies, and the conspiracy at Newburgh was not the first one for the American army. What was different about this mutiny was the person orchestrating it. The uprising did not come from the enlisted soldiers, but from the officers. Indeed, Gates was one of the highest ranking officers in the army.

Though most Americans at the time didn't know it, their beloved nation sat in grave peril. Not from the enemy, but from itself. Not from the outside, but the inside. The mutineers intended not only to get the money they were owed, but also to take over the young government itself. Who could stop such a movement? How could a group of armed men led by senior officers be denied? What could be done to save the fledgling nation from military rule?

Only one man could save America from its own army: George Washington.

One of history's ironies is that the man who led the American military had always wanted to be a British officer. Growing up in the British colony of Virginia, young George Washington first sought service in the British navy. His mother, however, vetoed the idea. Later, he joined the British Army. He was dismayed to find that the British officers held him in low regard because he was born on the wrong side of the Atlantic. Yet he served with great courage and conviction.

Washington was always growing as a leader. By the time he was twenty-six, he had fought in the French and Indian War, run a huge plantation, and served in the Virginia House of Burgesses. He was a man on the move.

When he arrived at the Continental Congress in 1775, he looked the part of a military leader. Literally. He wore a beautiful uniform. When Congress decided to chose a military commander, they had to look no farther than the man from Virginia. It was an inspired choice. Though Washington was not a great tactician, he proved to be a fine strategist.

Throughout the American Revolution, Washington had a keen appreciation for what later-day military strategists would call the "center of gravity," which is the military doctrine that a commander must always understand what his most important asset is and seek to protect it at all costs. The British mistakenly thought the Americans' center of gravity was their cities. The British seemed to think capture Boston, or perhaps New York City or Philadelphia, and the revolt would end.

Washington saw things differently. He believed the center of gravity was his own army. So long as his army stayed in the field, the revolution was alive. If his army was ever captured or destroyed, the struggle for independence would be over. Washington's strategy was simple—win by surviving. He avoided unnecessary skirmishes and he carefully chose his battles. In all, Washington only fought about nine battles throughout the entire war. But each day his army survived, America inched a little closer to victory. They could afford to wait it out. The British could not.

After he finally cornered and defeated the British at Yorktown in 1781, Washington's army stayed in the field awaiting a negotiated end to the war. Throughout the war, Washington carefully cultivated a sense of community among his men. He was one of them. He shared their hardships, their sufferings, and their battles. But now, with the war winding down and more time on their hands, the men got restless. They wanted to be paid. And they wanted to be paid now. It was a situation ripe with danger and ready for exploitation. The mutiny just might have prevailed until Washington discovered it.

On the morning of March 15, the officers met at the Public Building in Newburgh. With an actor's sense of timing and entrance, Washington arrived late and dramatically entered through a side door. What a pose he must have struck.

George Washington was big man. At six feet two inches, he towered over most of his contemporaries. Years of work on the land and riding a horse gave him a masculine, athletic physique. He looked every bit the handsome general in his perfectly tailored uniform. Yet for his many leadership skills, Washington was not a talker, and his speech that day in Newburgh at first fell flat. He urged the officers to refuse to join the mutiny. They were unmoved.

Washington pulled a letter, which was written by a Congressional ally, from his pocket. He paused and reached back into his pocket. The men leaned forward in their chairs to see what he was doing. The general pulled out a wiry device and began to unfold it. As he put on the reading glasses, he apologized to the men: "Gentlemen, you will permit me to put on my spectacles, for I have not only grown gray but almost blind in the service of my country."

Within seconds, tears filled the eyes of almost all the officers in the room. They had been so focused on their own sacrifice that they had forgotten about the sacrifice of others, including their general. What a price he had paid for all of them. After the meeting ended, no more talk of mutiny was ever heard. In his extraordinary life, Washington won many battles. But none more quickly or more decisively than at Newburgh, New York. With one sentence, marked by self-deprecating humor and humble honesty, Washington shamed the men who only moments before planned a military coup. How could they take over the government? Hadn't Washington suffered as much or more than any of them?

Washington paid an enormous price for fighting the British. It's hard for Americans today to realize the length of the American Revolutionary War. In our recent memory, World War II lasted four years. The Revolution lasted twice as long. For eight long years of fighting, Washington shouldered the responsibilities of command and the pressure to keep the Revolution alive. During this time, he was lucky if he saw his wife even once a year. At Valley Forge, he starved along with the men. That cold winter of 1777, there was sometimes only enough food for one day, leaving Washington and his men to worry about what they would eat the next day. Like his men, Washington weathered the frigid Pennsylvania winter in a hastily-constructed hut of wood. Not a day passed that he didn't feel the bitter sting of the cold. Through it all, for eight long years, he had to fight not only the British, but also the Congress. He constantly asked for better supplies, more pay for his troops, and an end to short-term enlistments. Washington was one of the richest men in Virginia when the war started. He had nothing to gain and everything to lose by fighting the British. Yet fight he did. And suffer. And sacrifice.

His message that day in Newburgh was this: Yes, he would help the men get justice from the Congress. But he would never abandon the cause of freedom for which he had fought. For Washington, the cause and the team were bigger than any one individual.

Few problems afflict America today more than the elevation of individual wants over community needs. To provide some perspective, Yale law professor Stephen L. Carter urges Americans to think of life as a journey on a railcar: "But if, as we now seem to think, there are no other passengers, there is no community, we can do what we like, not just on the roads but everywhere." He writes that the illusion of traveling alone is just that—an illusion. We all need each other. Too many Americans today travel the road of life alone, with little regard to how their actions will help or hurt those around them. Of course, this is not a phenomenon unique to Americans. Since the Garden of Eden, human nature has shown a desire to satisfy its own needs first and always.

Yet human nature has also shown the ability to express compassion about the station of others in life. Human beings are by definition social creatures. We not only like having friends and

17

neighbors, we need them. How much do we need others? When we get sick, we visit the doctor. When we want to learn, we attend school and study. When we want to start a business, we sell a product to customers. Interaction with others is part of life. So how do we create a sense of community? How do we remember that our journeys involve not just ourselves but others? The key is to direct our own interests to the interests of others; to use our talents and energies serving a cause greater than ourselves.

Think back to the story of Washington and his officers in 1783. The officers were not bad people. They just made a poor choice. They had a legitimate complaint. But they pursued it in an illegitimate fashion. And how did it happen? Because they thought about themselves instead of others; because they lost perspective and lost sight of the cause. With a little bit of leadership from their commander, they were able to return to a sense of team and do the right thing.

An army is a team, a community in arms. Soldiers are taught early that in order to protect themselves they must protect each other. These days, Army Rangers are famous for never leaving any of their own behind. Not the living, not the wounded, not the dead. Everyone is accounted for. This is how a team operates. By looking out for the interests of others, soldiers insure the protection of their own interests. After all, it might be you that gets wounded someday. Wouldn't you want someone to take care of you?

This is how the military works. But soldiers are humans—they make mistakes. When they do, they need leadership to point them back in the right direction. That's what Washington did. In his speech that March day to his men, he spoke of the "cause of our common country." He reminded them. "I have never left your side one moment," he said. Simply put, Washington was appealing to the men's sense of community. He was pointing out to the men his own commitment, which had been demonstrated during the war. But if his speech wasn't able to rekindle a spirit of team, the sight of his glasses did. No one had suffered more than Washington. No one had given more to the cause than Washington, and no one more completely tied up his own interests with the interests of the Revolution.

Throughout American history, great leaders have always immersed themselves in great causes. Indeed, they embodied the causes. When we think of the Revolution, we think of Washington. The Civil War? Abraham Lincoln. World War II? Franklin Delano Roosevelt. The civil rights movement? Dr. Martin Luther King, Jr.. These leaders were successful in part because they promoted a sense a community, a climate of team play, and a spirit of unity.

What a great lesson for us today. Before we think of ourselves, let's think of others. Before we point a finger, let's extend a hand. People who are caught up in a cause greater than themselves are too busy to get caught up blaming others or complaining about their own problems. As one of George Washington's contemporaries, Benjamin Franklin, once observed: "When you are good to others, you are best to yourself."

Make an effort to build a sense of community and a spirit of unity. Find a cause bigger than yourself. And if you see others losing their focus, show some leadership like Washington and bring them back into the fold. And above all, remember that when you bless others, you, too, will be blessed.

CHAPTER FOUR

WE VALUE SERVICE

"That all men are created equal."

—Declaration of Independence, 1776

THEY NUMBERED fifty-six. Lawyers. Business owners. Even a teacher. Some were world famous. Some would never be heard from again. They came from different places. Yet a common goal united them. A dream guided them to their destiny. A dream of all people in all nations—they wanted to be free.

In the spring of 1776, fifty-six Americans met in Philadelphia to find a way to explain to the world what they were fighting for in this new land. A committee was established to write out the reasons for their rebellion against the British Crown. Written largely by a young Thomas Jefferson, the Declaration of Independence was approved on July 4, 1776. Later that summer, each man signed his name on the document, right below the words pledging "our lives, our fortunes, and our sacred honor."

Most Americans know the story of how the Declaration of Independence came to life. But few know how the Declaration affected the lives of those who signed it. Indeed, they paid for their rebellion with their lives, fortunes, and honor. The fifty-six signers of the Declaration of Independence served others by sacrificing themselves.

Abraham Clark sacrificed for the cause not with his life but with his family. A New Jersey man who signed the document, he didn't have the luxury of offering his life for his country. Instead, he bore the cruel burden of watching his sons suffer for the cause.

Both his sons served in the American army and were captured by the British. They were tortured because of their father's signature on the Declaration of Independence. Still, the British made Abraham Clark a simple offer. They would spare his sons if he would renounce the rebellion. Clark refused. He was willing to let his sons suffer so that his young country could live.

Thomas Nelson, Jr. of Virginia sacrificed his home for the cause. During the battle of Yorktown, Nelson's home was seized by the British and used as the headquarters for General Charles Cornwallis. During the battle, Nelson became enraged when he learned that American artillery officers had refrained from attacking his house. "Give me the cannon," he reportedly said. He then shelled his own house until it was destroyed. Years later, he died an impoverished man at the age of fifty having never recovered from the destruction of his property.

Arthur Middleton sacrificed for the cause with his personal liberty. When the British overran Charleston in 1781, this native South Carolinian was taken prisoner. In the meantime, Middleton's fortune was ruined. When he emerged from prison at the end of the war, he was broke, but not broken. He possessed the courage of his convictions. He had carried himself with honor and dignity, even willingly suffering in prison for the cause of freedom.

Joseph Hewes sacrificed for the cause with his own life. After signing the Declaration of Independence, he worked tirelessly on behalf of the revolution. A shipping magnate in North Carolina, Hewes placed his ships into the service of the Continental Armed Forces. He also served ably in the Continental Congress as the Secretary of the Naval Affairs Committee. Undoubtedly, the stress and hard work took their toll on the man. In 1779, he became gravely ill and died shortly thereafter at the age of fifty not knowing if his cause would prevail.

These are the men of Philadelphia—the leaders of the American Revolution and the heroes of our founding. Some sacrificed their fortunes, many lost their lives, still others gave their children. In all, nine of the fifty-six signers died during the war. Five others found themselves in prison where they were often beaten and starved by the enemy. Twelve had their homes burned to the ground, and seventeen others lost all their possessions.

The fifty-six men who signed the Declaration of Independence did more than pledge their lives. They gave their lives, their homes, and their children. They suffered so that others might be free. They put meaning into the words of this most important document. More than two hundred years later, the story of these brave Americans is sometimes forgotten, but their impact remains. Even now, in dark nights and quiet days, we can hear the voices of these men echoing across the years. These voices whisper to us to stand strong. They remind us that America is only free so long as Americans are brave. After all, the liberty of America is always, and only, the product of the courage of Americans. The road to a better tomorrow is paved today by those willing to serve and sacrifice for a noble cause.

Many of these men died for others. Why were they so willing to suffer, to sacrifice, and even to die? They did it because there are some things were fighting for, dying for, and even worth living for.

From the time of our founding until today, Americans have always been willing to sacrifice for others. Our story is the story of many people coming together to help each other. The reason we have always been willing to serve is that we have been committed to a cause greater than ourselves. Our motto says it best: "Out of many, one." For more than two hundred years, we have been diverse but united; we have been a country of individuals who come together to form a nation of one people. Like a river flowing toward the sea, we gain strength and power from other streams and rivers that connect with us and form as one.

Today, long after the American Revolution, Americans from every walk of life and every corner of America continue to serve their nation by serving their neighbors. Unlike the heroes of 1776, most of us will never be asked to die for others. But we are asked to live for others.

So how do we do it? How do we build a better community where more people serve each other?

To begin with, serving others means having the courage to care. In today's society it's easy to hide behind the comforts of modernity. It takes courage and commitment for people to notice those around them and take a stand on issues important to their neighbors. Nobel Prize Winner and Holocaust survivor Elie Weisel once remarked that the opposite of love is not hate, but indifference. The German people didn't necessarily hate the Jews during World War II. They just didn't care. Or they didn't care enough. Because they didn't care, millions of people died. The first step in creating a society where people serve is to create a society where people care.

This is what the great British statesman Edmund Burke meant when he said all that is necessary for evil to prevail is for good men to do nothing. Here in America, we have always found good people willing to give something for their neighbors and nation. This is a sacred tradition that we must protect and preserve; it's like an ancestral home that we must care for so that our children may one day inherit it. More than information or knowledge, people need to feel the magic that comes from being around a kind and caring person. If we seek to help someone in need, we must first seek to know and care about that person.

Second, serving others means a commitment to taking action. Not just doing something, but doing something meaningful. Not just doing things right, but doing the right thing. The writer Ernest Hemingway pointed out there is a difference between motion and action. Action means actually doing something that makes a difference. The heroes of 1776 weren't just going through the motions and keeping busy. What did they do? They made history while helping to make America free. How did they do it? By fighting and sacrificing for others. Difference-making, not busywork, is the meaning of service.

Third, serving others means believing in a cause greater than ourselves. Many men have signed declarations throughout history. Many have fought in revolutions. And most are forgotten in history. Why are the men of 1776 remembered today? Why is Jefferson's masterpiece studied all around the world today? Why did the protesters in China's Tiananmen Square in 1989 quote the words of our Declaration of Independence? The document has endured because its principles are universal and transcend the American nation herself. Our Founding Fathers understood that only by fighting for a worthy cause could they ever hope to claim victory over a mighty enemy. So they found their cause—the cause of freedom—and they enlisted their services in that cause.

How do we emulate the spirit of 1776? It takes the courage to care, a commitment to act, and a cause bigger than ourselves.

Where do we start? Just take a look around you. There are pockets of despair in every town and streets of loneliness in every community.

Countless ways exist for you to help those around you. Here are just three:

In 2001, the U.S. Census Bureau reported that more than 11 percent of the U.S. population lived below the poverty line. That means one out of every ten people you see may be poor and hungry. Volunteer at your local food bank. Gather cans of food. Collect donations. These actions can help feed the hungry in your neighborhood or community.

Meanwhile, there are more than 1.5 million elderly Americans living in nursing homes. They need a friend. Take some time out of your schedule and spend a weekend at your local nursing home.

The scourge of alcohol and drugs continues to plague this nation. Federal government statistics show that alcohol is involved in 71 percent of all murders, 41 percent of all assaults, 50 percent of all rapes, 60 percent of all sex crimes committed against children, 60 percent of all child abuse cases, and 55 percent of arrests overall. How can you help? Volunteer your time at a drug prevention program at your church or in your community.

Helping those who are hungry, elderly, and afflicted by drugs or alcohol is a wonderful way to serve a cause greater than yourself. There are many other ways as well. Coach Little League. Give blood. Tutor a young student. The list is endless. Each time you provide help and hope to those in need you commit yourself to one of the most powerful forces that makes America work—service.

Where else in the world do sixty-three million people volunteer in one form or another to help their fellow countrymen? In 2003, according to the USA Freedom Corps, that's exactly how many people gave their time to help someone. Astounding, but that's America.

It's a good thing so many people offer help. We need them. America has the world's freest economy, but a free economy means some people won't do as well as others. That's always a hazard of a free system, but that's why service is so important. Service helps fill in the gaps for those who have been left out and left behind. To ensure our freedom, we must ensure that we have safeguards to help out everyone. Serving others is that safeguard. Besides, by volunteering we help ourselves and we give meaning to our lives. Serving others not only makes America work, it makes America great.

SECTION TWO

LIBERTY

CHAPTER FIVE

WE VALUE EQUALITY

"We must learn to live together as brothers or perish together as fools."

—Dr. Martin Luther King, Jr., 1964

H E WOULD LATER CALL THEM the "longest hours" of his life.

As the doors closed on him, he was isolated, but not alone. Others surrounded him, but they wore uniforms and angry faces. They were not his friends.

For many years now, this had been his lot: leaning against the steel walls and sleeping on the concrete floor. Prison was many things. But for Dr. Martin Luther King, Jr., one thing it was not was new. Now, for the thirteenth time since he entered the national consciousness in 1956, King found himself in jail.

This would be hard on anyone, but it was especially hard on King. According to his friend and colleague, Andrew Young, King always feared prison because no witnesses, no cameras, and no help of any kind existed behind locked doors. In jail, racist cops could have their way with him. In fact, they often did.

Yet, King persevered. He found a certain redemptive power in unjust suffering. By going to jail, he showed the nation and the world that he would pay any price to help equality truly come to America. As he often said, "the ultimate measure of a man is not where he stands in moments of comfort and convenience, but where he stands at times of challenge and controversy."

As he lay down that night in his cell, he must have thought about what had happened and how it would all play out; he must have wondered about the movement's future and why so many had to suffer so much to receive something so simple—equality.

During the next few days King's friends and family brought scraps of paper to his prison cell. He collected them while collecting his thoughts. King was always able to find the good in the bad, to turn "dark yesterdays into bright tomorrows." Now he would seek to explain the meaning of his suffering. He would transcend the iron bonds of imprisonment and reach for the velvet chords of love that he believed could unite all Americans.

He took his pen and began to write.

He would write a new chapter in the story of America. Literally. He would write the most important defense of American freedom and equality since the Gettysburg Address in 1863.

◇

What had led King to this moment? Why was he in jail yet again? In 1963, King's heart was in Birmingham, Alabama but his mind focused on Washington. He had come to believe that new national legislation was needed to ensure equal treatment of blacks in public places. Inspired by President John F. Kennedy's words but discouraged by his lack of action, King decided to try and force the president's hand. He would raise the stakes by staging a mass protest in Birmingham. He would show the president, and the nation, just how urgently a civil rights bill was needed. He previously told the president that the "key to everything is federal commitment." He now intended to show him why.

Throughout the 1960s, the strategy of the civil rights movement followed a familiar pattern. King would target a Southern city for a protest, bring increased media attention to the injustices present there, and then watch as the Southern leaders began to feel the pressure of the national spotlight. Once they were ready to deal, King would gladly attempt to reach an agreement. Some civil rights leaders felt King didn't demand enough in some of the negotiations. As Andrew Young later wrote, King's strategy was to create a "new relationship between people black and white." He wanted to convert the city's leaders, not humiliate them.

Birmingham proved to be a much tougher battle. King deliberately focused the protest on the city's economic power-brokers, but they showed no signs of feeling the pressure of the national media spotlight. Indeed, the business leaders cheered as Birmingham Police Commissioner Bull Connor gladly began arresting protestors and sending them to jail.

Yet King knew that the more people who were arrested the longer the story would stay in the news and the more pressure would increase on the leaders in Birmingham and Washington.

Like all great generals, King believed he belonged at the front with his troops. In April 1963, he went to jail in Birmingham for the cause.

In jail his lawyers brought him of a copy of a recent *Birmingham News* newspaper. In it, King read a public statement signed by a group of white ministers. The statement praised the police and urged King and others to stop the protest and seek their cause in court. King decided to respond in spectacular fashion. King's "Letter From Birmingham Jail" would become a classic in American literature.

Written on those pieces and scraps of paper brought to him by friends, the letter contained King's entire thoughts on equality and the meaning of the civil rights movement. King first established his credentials. The white ministers previously complained about "outsiders" coming to Birmingham. King reminded them that "injustice anywhere is a threat to justice everywhere." He then described the sense of urgency that he and others brought with them to Birmingham. "Freedom is never voluntarily given by the oppressor; it must be demanded by the oppressed."

But the heart of the message, and its true genius, rested in its exposition of the meaning of equality and the horrors of inequality. "Perhaps it is easy for those who have never felt the stinging darts of segregation to say, 'Wait,'" he wrote. King answered with a story about his daughter Yoki:

"When you suddenly find your tongue twisted and your speech stammering as you seek to explain to your six-year-old daughter why she can't go to the public amusement park...then you will understand why we find it difficult to wait."

King's letter, smuggled out by his lawyers, became an instant classic. As historian Stephen Oates noted, the white ministers never responded. King's letter was "unanswerable."

That's because King's reasoning was unimpeachable. Throughout his career, King was very careful to always place the pursuit of equality in the context of the American story. King argued that racism existed not because of America's principles, but in spite of America's principles. He believed segregation constituted a sin that went against America's values. At the March on Washington in 1963, he talked about the great wells of democracy "dug deep by the Founding Fathers." From these wells of equality he sought to draw upon. He felt that the vision of the Founding Fathers should be extended to every American from every walk of life. After all, hadn't Thomas Jefferson written that "all men are created equal"?

King once said that "we must learn to live together as brothers or perish together as fools." He lived for the cause of equality. And, five years after Birmingham, he died for it.

<>

Equality is often-talked-about. Women's rights activists talk about equal pay. Minority leaders speak about equal rights. Political scientists study Congress and worry about equal representation. A lot of people have volumes to say about equality. But what did the Founding Fathers have to say about it?

Quite a bit, it turns out. But their view of equality may surprise you.

For the Founding Fathers, the challenge of creating a new nation offered the chance to correct the errors of their British ancestors. Wealthy landowners and prominent families came first in England, and people in colonies came last. Indeed, George Washington himself experienced this lack of opportunity when he tried to make a career in the British army.

The Founders sought to level the playing field. They sought not an equality of outcomes, but an equality of opportunity. Thomas Jefferson, the author of the American Declaration of Independence, wrote to his friend John Adams that "there is a natural Aristocracy among men; the grounds of which are Virtue and Talents."

In other words, America would replace the British aristocracy of wealth and privilege with a new aristocracy of talent and ability. In the new nation, anyone could achieve anything.

Of course, the invention of America was not perfect. From the start, America failed to deliver on its promise of equality to all its citizens. Women would have to wait. So would the poor. And, most infamously, so would the millions of blacks who lived in bondage as slaves.

Jefferson himself worried about this contradiction. "I tremble for my country," he once wrote about slavery, "when I reflect that God is just." Yet Jefferson remained in possession of slaves until the day he died.

But God is just. The moment of reckoning Jefferson feared did come with the bloody Civil War. Still, even after that war life was anything but equal for blacks. Decades of Jim Crow destroyed hopes; years of lynching instilled fears.

Out of this darkness emerged the light of the civil rights movement. King demanded simply, and only, that America live by its principles. That meant equal opportunity. Equal opportunity to work, to vote, and to pursue the American dream.

Today we sometimes confuse people having equal rights with people having equal things. This may be a legitimate viewpoint but not necessarily the Founding Fathers' viewpoint. They believed America would be a place where different people would achieve different things. Government's role was to simply create a fair environment where everyone could use his or her "virtue and talents." This was the natural aristocracy they hoped to achieve, and this is the America we inherit and live in today.

Still, we can all do more to help create a more perfect union and a more equal society. Perhaps education is equality's best friend. By doing more for our schools and asking more from our teachers, we can produce graduates who are ready to achieve according to their "virtue and talents."

If you are a parent, and you want your child to succeed, take an interest in his or her schoolwork and visit the school to talk to teachers.

If you are a teacher, find new ways to challenge your students. Give them extra assignments, send them on field trips, and teach them that learning is fun.

And if you are a student, remember that what you learn now will benefit you later. Success favors the prepared and the educated. Be ready for your future.

Whoever you are and wherever you are, always remember to look out for others. Get what you want in life by helping others get what they want in life.

CHAPTER SIX

WE VALUE JUSTICE

*"We are caught in an inescapable network of mutuality,
tied in a single garment of destiny."*

—Dr. Martin Luther King, Jr., 1963

SHE WASN'T TRYING to make a stand. She was just trying to take a seat.

The first of December, 1955 dawned cold and gray in the city of Montgomery, Alabama. As the day progressed, people tended to their stores or worked in their offices, waiting until it was time to go home.

At a bus stop in downtown Montgomery, the actions of a quiet woman were about to be heard around the world. A seamstress who was tired and ready to go home waited patiently for the bus. Little did she know this would be a ride that would take her into history.

◇

For blacks, life in the 1950s South was filled with fear. Fear of their white neighbors, the police, and the law itself. These were the days of Jim Crow where America was separate and unequal. With the infamous *Plessy v. Ferguson* Supreme Court decision in 1896, white Southerners established a caste system of rules that gave blacks equal rights but not to equal things. Blacks could attend a movie theater, but they had to sit in the balcony. Black children could receive a public education but at different schools than white children. And blacks could ride on the bus but not in the same seats as whites.

These rules created a climate of anxiety, resentment, and anger. How could a nation founded on the principle that "all men are created equal" treat an entire group of citizens so unequally?

In 1954, a ray of light broke through the dark clouds of American segregation. The Supreme Court ruled in *Brown v. the Board of Education* that separate but equal in public schools meant separate but unequal. They ruled that schools must desegregate. Yet they merely urged states and school districts to do so with "deliberate speed." It turned out, speed was relative. Change occurred slowly in the South.

With their hopes raised and dashed again, black Southerners' discontent continued to smolder. They were frustrated that America refused to live the meaning of the Declaration of Independence.

They wondered: Who would lead them? Who could change the minds of the American people? Who might take the lead and help start a movement that could change the South and change history?

Her name was Rosa Parks.

◇

Seamstresses work hard hours. And that December day was a long day for Rosa Parks. As she got onto the bus that afternoon, she was tired, even exhausted. She would later say that she was mainly tired of the injustice she endured. Her eyes were heavy yet sharp enough to notice that she recognized the driver of the bus. He was an angry man who had thrown her off his bus once because she had refused to enter through the back door of the bus.

Undaunted, she stepped onto the bus. Contrary to what most people have read or heard about this story, Mrs. Parks did not sit in the front part of the bus. Instead, not trying to cause a scene, she sat with a man who was next to the window. This was a seat that blacks were allowed to use.

But all that changed as more passengers entered the bus. At the third bus stop, a white man was left standing. The driver told three black passengers to give up their seats. Two stood up and walked to the back of the bus. Few remember their names, but no one will ever forget the woman who refused to stand.

The bus driver immediately threatened Mrs. Parks. "I'll have you arrested," he forcefully told her. She told him to go ahead with his threat. He did. Within a few minutes, the police arrived. An officer approached Mrs. Parks and asked her why she wouldn't move. Rather than answer, she posed a question to the office: "Why do you push us around?" The officer said "the law is the law and you are under arrest."

Within minutes, the police took Parks off the bus and placed her into the police car. The story of her arrest was just the beginning. And America would never be the same again.

<>

She wasn't the first person ever to be arrested on a city bus. But Rosa Parks was different. She was a very prominent, well-known, and well-respected member of the black community in Montgomery, having once served as a staff member for the president of the local National Association for the Advancement of Colored People. Thanks to Rosa Parks, with her dignity, grace, and courage, Americans would not be able to look away from the issue of segregation again.

Within days of her arrest, the first wave of the Montgomery bus boycott began. Outraged black citizens of Montgomery walked, rode bikes, or carpooled to work rather than ride the city's buses. For three hundred and eighty one days, they continued their boycott. Finally, on November 13, 1956, the Supreme Court struck down city and state laws in Alabama that allowed segregated busing. Five weeks later, the buses officially desegregated. That day, a young minister who had helped organize and lead the Montgomery bus boycott took his place in the front seat of a city bus. His name was Dr. Martin Luther King, Jr.

Why did people like Rosa Parks and Dr. Martin Luther King, Jr. risk everything to improve the lives of Southern blacks? "Injustice anywhere is a threat to justice everywhere," King famously explained. "We are caught in an inescapable network of mutuality, tied in a single garment of destiny."

For King, the civil rights movement was about more than the rights of blacks. It was about the rights of all. It was more than getting a seat on the bus; it was getting a piece of the American Dream. And it was more than just preventing injustice somewhere in Alabama, it was about promoting justice everywhere in America.

As the examples of Parks and King demonstrate, justice is not just a concept that law professors seek to define; it is defined every day when ordinary people use their rights to help others.

<>

From the very beginning of the American republic, a sense of justice has inspired and encouraged our people. Indeed, the heroes of the American Revolution were in large part motivated by the injustices of their relationship with the British. "No taxation without representation" was not a slogan for economic reform but a cry for justice. Thomas Jefferson's list of sins committed by the British, which are found in the Declaration of Independence, serves as an eloquent complaint to the world. It shows that America had a just cause in revolting because Americans had been denied justice in the colonies.

More than two hundred years later, this same sense of justice continues to guide American leaders through the dust and din of world events. Who else but America would seek to replace the Taliban government in Afghanistan with a democratically-elected government? And who else but Americans would seek to help the people of Iraq set up a system of laws and courts to protect the rights of all?

Yet what is truly unique about America is that our sense of justice is not limited to government. Yes, we have courts of law and police to protect the rights of all. We have city halls, state legislatures, and the Congress to pass laws to deal with important issues of fairness to the citizens of this country.

The real sense of justice—the real power of fairness—is found not in our government but in our people. Indeed, many times, the courts and the legislatures simply ratify the changes that have been brought about by people of good will.

Rosa Parks did not wait on a court ruling before she boarded that bus in Montgomery. Indeed, her action forced the courts to consider the case and issue a ruling. Thus, in the case of Parks, as with so many other leaders of the civil rights movement, it was an American citizen, more than an American institution, that led the way to a more humane, more just society.

<>

Simply put, one of the things that make America great is its sense of justice rests with its people. We don't have to wait for a ruling from a court to know when something is wrong. We don't have to hear the speech of a president to know how to make something right.

Read the story of America's history and it's the story of American people acting out for justice.

When Susan B. Anthony, a leader in the women's rights movement of the nineteenth century, was told she couldn't vote because she was a woman, she saw an injustice and acted. Thanks to her, woman's suffrage became the law of the land.

When Florence Kelley, a social worker, witnessed the appalling conditions of child labor in factories, she saw an injustice and she acted. Her book *Our Toiling Children* helped bring about new protections in the law for child workers.

And when a King heard about the arrest of Parks, he saw an injustice and he acted.

The Old Testament states that promoting justice means doing right and loving mercy. It has been so for the American people since 1776. Our sense of justice is predicated on the ability of our people to see a wrong and make it right; to see those in need and have mercy and compassion for them.

Here in this blessed land, the power of our justice is found in our people more than our government. This is what makes our system of justice so effective, so powerful, and so inspiring to people everywhere. After all, it works here, and it can work anywhere in the world.

CHAPTER SEVEN

WE VALUE COMPASSION

"With malice toward none, with charity for all."

—Abraham Lincoln, 1865

AMID THE SMOKE AND DIN OF BATTLE, few noticed the boat pulling up the James River and docking just south of Richmond. Why would they? A battle brewed. The stakes were high. The drama even higher.

This was Virginia in March, 1865 where the great American Civil War was reaching a climax.

To the south, General William Tecumseh Sherman was pummeling the Confederate Army of General Joseph E. Johnston. To the east of Richmond, General Ulysses Grant prepared his final assault of General Robert E. Lee's grand army of northern Virginia. After nearly four years of war and 600,000 casualties, America's bloodiest chapter was writing its final few sentences.

As Grant and Sherman made their plans, a visitor arrived in a boat called the River Queen. He wanted to help write a happy ending to this sad chapter of American history. The script he had in mind would only enhance his esteemed place in history.

◇

For Abraham Lincoln, the Civil War was a brutal, personal struggle. Perhaps no wartime leader has ever personally suffered as much as Lincoln. His wife's Southern relatives had worn the gray and fought against him. His precious young son, Willie, died at the White House. His wife was not always stable. As if those troubles weren't enough, he suffered defeat after defeat on the battlefield.

The man who promised in his first inaugural address that he had no qualms with the South—indeed he said "we are friends, not enemies"—had faced four years of horrific violence. When his troops were famously routed at Chancellorsville in 1863, Lincoln, stunned and staggered by the news, openly asked those around him: "My God, my God. What will the country say?"

The country said a good deal, and that added to Lincoln's misery. He was pilloried by the press, savaged by his congressional enemies, and doubted by countless Americans. People asked: How could someone run such an incompetent war?.

Yet for all the shortcomings of the war, one constant remained through it all—Lincoln's resolve. As the storms mounted around him, he was the anchor that rallied the Union cause. When others took cover, he took action. Decisively. Relentlessly. And rightfully.

As the war began, Lincoln clung to the hope that he could fight to simply repair the Union. Soon, he realized that too many lives were being sacrificed to justify a mere reunion with the South. To win the war, he would have to free the slaves.

And so he did. Lincoln brilliantly turned the political tide on the South by moralizing the Civil War. He never looked back. As battlefield losses grew, so too did Lincoln's resolve. "We cannot escape history," Lincoln told Congress, "we will be remembered in spite of ourselves." Lincoln was determined to be remembered as the president who risked everything—his country, his troops, his office, even his life—to free the slaves and save the Union.

Slowly, the winds of fate began to blow Lincoln's way. At Gettysburg, Union troops turned back Lee's vaunted army in the largest land battle ever held on American soil. As the 1864 election approached, Lincoln received more good news from the front—Sherman took Atlanta, and Farragaut took Mobile Bay. In

November 1864, Lincoln beat his Democratic opponent George B. McClellan and won a hard fought reelection victory that all but assured the Union would finish the job and end the war.

But how would it end the war? Many of Lincoln's fellow Republicans were breathing vengeful threats on the South. After all, didn't that make sense? Doesn't there have to be a punishment to fit the crime? Weren't the Southerners guilty of not only inhumanity to the slaves but treason to their country?

As rumors swirled about how the post-war South would look, and as Grant and Sherman prepared to destroy the remainder of the Confederate armies facing them, Lincoln decided to go for a boat ride. He left Washington and headed for Virginia. Having all but won the war, he was determined to win the peace. And his idea of how to treat the defeated Southerners would surprise a lot of people including the Southerners.

<>

As Lincoln journeyed down the Chesapeake Bay toward Richmond, perhaps he reflected on his recent inauguration. In his second inaugural address, Lincoln spoke about the painful wounds the nation had suffered. He spoke the words that so perfectly captured both his determination to vanquish his opponents and his humanity to those vanquished:

"With malice toward none; with charity for all; with firmness in the right, as God gives us to see the right, let us strive on to finish the work we are in; to bind up the nation's wounds; to care for him who shall have borne the battle, and for his widow and his orphan...to do all which may achieve and cherish a just and lasting peace among ourselves and with all nations."

Many Americans no doubt assumed that Lincoln's words were directed to Northerners. After all, they were the ones who had sacrificed so much to end slavery and save the Union. It was their wounds that would need to be healed. It was their families who needed care. It turns out Lincoln's vision was bigger than just the North.

<>

On March, 24, 1865, Generals Grant and Sherman along with Admiral David Dixon Porter boarded the *River Queen*. For the next few hours the military leaders spoke about their plans to strike a final, devastating blow to the Southern armies. But soon, the conversation turned to the end game. What would happen when the cannons were silenced and the guns were quiet?

At this point, Lincoln openly discussed his plans for reconstruction. To their surprise, he urged the officers to offer "liberal and honorable" terms of surrender to the Confederate armies still in the fields. He also wanted them to offer a general amnesty for participants in the rebellion as well as immediate restoration of citizenship for the Southerners. Finally, he wanted to begin the work of creating a gradual transition of state governments to the South.

Perhaps the most revealing moment in the meeting came when the military leaders asked Lincoln about the future of the leaders of the Confederate government. If Jefferson Davis, president of the Confederacy, was to be captured, there would be enormous pressure for the Union to hang him. Reverting to his favorite habit, Lincoln chose to answer this difficult question with a simple story. He spoke of the teetotaler who went to a party and asked for a glass of lemonade. When the server asked him if wanted his lemonade spiked, the man replied that he wouldn't mind it as long as he didn't know about it. Lincoln paused, allowed the impact of the story to settle on the men in the room, and said no more. The military leaders left the meeting convinced that the point of Lincoln's story was that it wouldn't be bad if Jefferson Davis escaped the country as long as Lincoln didn't know about it.

As the meeting ended, the men in uniform must have been amazed by the generous tone and spirit of their wartime leader. Here was a man who had given everything but his life—and that too would come—to win this war. Yet, here in his great moment of triumph, he spoke of reconciliation, not retaliation.

A few days later, Richmond fell. As Lee's army made one last, desperate attempt to retreat and fight again, Lincoln decided to view the destroyed city for himself. With his son Tad at his side, he walked among the ruins of Richmond. A few Union sympathizers greeted him on the street and urged Lincoln to punish the Confederates. "Judge not," Lincoln responded, "lest you be judged."

On April 9, Lee surrendered to Grant at Appomattox. He received the generous terms that Lincoln had instructed Grant to offer. Four days later, Lincoln discussed his reconstruction plan with his cabinet, and then went to Ford's Theater to see *My American Cousin*. He was shot in the back of the head by John Wilkes Booth, a Southern sympathizer. The next morning, he died. And with him died the hopes of a generous and compassionate reconstruction policy.

<>

It was because of Lincoln's genius that he was able to simultaneously wage a relentless war on the South even though he had no anger against the Southerners. As someone who had suffered many hardships and setbacks in his life, Lincoln was an inherently compassionate man. Today, we often think of compassion as a matter of pocket change. But true compassion is about real change—the kind of change that comes from someone who cares about the suffering around him and reaches out to help. Lincoln truly cared about the South. He believed that "charity for all" also meant for the South. Their wounds needed healing as well as the North's. A vengeful reconstruction policy would only infect the wounds even more. Lincoln viewed the post-war period as a time of great opportunity—there had been so much suffering, which meant that so much good could be accomplished. Lincoln intended to do just that. What a cruel irony that an assassin's bullet robbed the North of their greatest leader and the South of its best friend.

◇

In a world too often filled with evil men and evil intentions, those people and those nations of goodwill stand out. Perhaps no event more vividly demonstrated this than September 11, 2001. What possessed nineteen men to overtake four planes and use them to wreak havoc on thousands of innocents? Only evil. What can overcome it? Only good—kindness, decency, and yes, compassion. Think of the countless Americans who waited in line to give blood after September 11. Think of the firefighters who went into the buildings to save others. Remember the stories of employees in the World Trade Center carrying disabled coworkers down the stairs to safety. Compassion is the glow of light that warms the cold of life.

But compassion doesn't just happen; it has to be chosen. Too often in history, compassion has been nowhere. In the 1930s, many people failed to recognize the Nazi menace because they failed to appreciate the realness of Adolf Hitler's evil. After the war, General Dwight D. Eisenhower ordered German civilians to tour the remains of the Holocaust sites—this kind of wickedness could only be believed by being seen.

Perhaps those Germans witnessing the remains of the Holocaust wondered how the Nazis could have so little compassion.

But America is not immune to such evil, either. At the very birth of this great republic, the curse of slavery was sanctioned in our law. Only a brutal, bloody civil war could end the iniquity that so many Americans had justified. Yet, the Civil War in many ways provides a perfect case study of how evil is handled in America. Slavery was wrong, but ending it was right regardless of the cost. America remains the only nation in history that fought a civil war among its own people to end slavery.

Lincoln realized that in confronting slavery, America must convert the slaver owner. To replace the slave society with a just society, Lincoln knew Southerners needed help, not hassles, an extended hand, not a pointed finger. Lincoln believed Southerners needed compassion.

Lincoln's policies were designed to create a better America. The Homestead Act allowed more Americans to have a place to live and a home to own. The Land Grand College Act helped Americans receive a college education. The Emancipation Proclamation ended slavery once and for all. Lincoln didn't just want to end evil; he wanted to replace it with compassion.

Throughout American history, compassion has always been more than a word. It has been a call to action. Today in Iraq, Americans are building hospitals and schools.

Columnist Charles Krauthammer notes that America is exceptional in its approach toward a country that it has overtaken militarily. History records that the Romans and the British did not have exit strategies. When they invaded a country, they planned to stay. Not so with America. As soon as possible, American troops in Iraq looked for ways to help rebuild the country so the citizens of Iraq could run it themselves.

On a more personal level, compassion is the way we all make the world a little better place every day. But compassion isn't a feeling; it's an action. It's the difference between *feeling* good and *doing* good. It's not an internal emotion; it's an external act. Anywhere and everywhere, real compassion means taking action.

Compassion isn't seeing someone homeless and feeling sorry for them. Compassion is taking that person to a homeless shelter.

Compassion isn't reading in the paper about the unemployed and saying, "That's too bad." Compassion is helping them find work.

And compassion isn't hearing about the number of students who have dropped out of your local school and wishing it weren't so. Compassion is organizing a program to get kids back in school and teach them the skills they will need to stay there.

Compassion is a great gift that all Americans should share with those around them. Want to make your community a little better place? Have some compassion and take some action.

CHAPTER EIGHT

WE VALUE RELIGIOUS FREEDOM

"Thus building a wall of separation between church and state."

—Thomas Jefferson, 1802

FOR BAPTISTS, 1801 WAS NOT A GOOD YEAR. At least not in Danbury, Connecticut. The good members of the Danbury Baptist Association were proud patriots living in a proud new nation. They believed in the American promise of religious freedom, and they were committed to exercising this right. Yet in their home state they were second-class citizens. Literally.

At that time, the state of Connecticut had an official state-sanctioned church, the Congregationalists. Because of this, more than just a stigma was placed on Baptists and other denominations. It also meant that a financial burden was placed on them because their tax dollars helped to pay for the official church. To many people, this mixture of religion and government had motivated them to leave Europe and journey to America in the first place.

Taunted by their neighbors and taxed by the government, the Baptists found themselves in a New World but facing the persecution of the Old World. What was worse was that they were confused. What they experienced daily did not seem consistent with the Constitution, which so many had heard about and a few had even read.

Didn't the Constitution guarantee the right to assembly? The right to free speech? More importantly, didn't it guarantee that Congress would make "no laws" restricting worship and that a government-sanctioned church would not be allowed?

Confused and concerned, the Danbury Baptist Association decided to take action. They decided to do something that countless Americans have done countless times over the years.

They decided to write a letter to President Thomas Jefferson.

◇

Jefferson called his own election to the presidency the "Revolution of 1800." For some politicians, this was mere political rhetoric. But when spoken by the author of the Declaration of Independence, it took on new meaning.

Jefferson believed America was heading down a dangerous path during the four years of John Adams' presidency. Adams was the very embodiment of New England religiosity—he was both moral and a moralizer. Sixty years later Lincoln would say that he hoped he was on God's side. Adams would have disagreed. Adams believed God was on his side. Indeed, Adams was all too willing to make Jefferson's religion—or the perceived lack of it—a key issue in the campaign.

History has been kinder to Adams' presidency than the American people were. In 1800, a majority opted for a new direction and a new president. In choosing the populism of the Democratic Republicans over the elitism of the Federalists, the American people started a political revolution, one that sought to return the country to the principles of its founding that inspired people across the country, even in Danbury, Connecticut.

◇

The members of the Danbury Baptist Association keenly observed the 1800 election. They saw what was happening in their part of New England, and they feared for their country. They found themselves cheering for Jefferson, the man who, after all, had told the world that everyone had "inalienable rights" that came from "their Creator." Yes, Jefferson was a man who believed in God, but beyond that, his views were unknown. This suited the Danbury Baptists just fine. In fact, this was exactly what they wanted—a man of faith, not a man of a particular church, in the new White House.

With this in mind, they wrote a letter to Jefferson in October 1801.

This began one of the most important and misunderstood exchanges of letters in American history. These letters forever changed the relationship between government and churches. And the debate begun then is one that continues today.

<>

As supporters of Jefferson, the members of the Danbury Baptist Association wasted no time describing their concern in their congratulatory letter :

"Our Sentiments are uniformly on the side of Religious Liberty—That Religion is at all times and places a Matter between God and Individuals—That no man ought to suffer in Name, person or effects on account of his religious Opinions—That the legitimate Power of civil Government extends no further than to punish the man who works ill to his neighbour."

Simply put, their argument was: We want to be left alone to worship God as we see fit. We don't believe it right for the government to treat us differently and use our tax dollars to fund another church.

As bold as this letter was, the Danbury Baptists believed they knew enough about Jefferson to ensure a favorable response.

In early 1802, Jefferson responded. His answer included one of the most quoted, and most misused, metaphors in American history.

"I contemplate with sovereign reverence," Jefferson wrote, "that act [the First Amendment] of the whole American people which declared that their legislature should 'make no law re-specting an establishment of religion, or prohibiting the free ex-ercise thereof,' thus building a wall of separation between Church & State."

Thus began the outline of the fabled wall-separated church and state. To this day, many Americans believe the phrase is found in the Constitution. It is not. Or in the Declaration of In-dependence. Not at all. Instead the words first appeared in a simple letter written from a thankful president to some of his staunch supporters.

Since these words are often the subject of controversy, it makes sense to reconsider the context of the conversation.

What made the Danbury Baptists complain? Their state had an established, official church, and they were discouraged from freely practicing their beliefs.

What was Jefferson's response? While sidestepping the issue of the Connecticut law, Jefferson quoted the First Amendment and agreed with the Danbury Baptists that the federal govern-ment should not ever operate an official church and it should never prevent citizens from expressing their faith anywhere and everywhere.

Thus, Jefferson's wall between church and state meant something very different than what we consider today. To Jef-ferson, a wall between church and state meant the freedom of religion, not freedom from religion.

◇

The American house is built upon a strong foundation with many bricks. One of the essential pieces of mortar holding up our nation is our sense of religious freedom. America is unique in its founding and its history. In many ways, we were to be both a people of faith and a government of no religion. This seemed like a contradiction to many in the world at the time of our founding, and it has been a source of confusion ever since. Simply put, from its beginning, this nation was to encourage religious freedom. But from the start this nation was not to sanction any official religion or discriminate against people of any faith.

As the Founding Fathers designed an intricate system of checks and balances, they faced a problem—how to balance the rights of the majority with the rights of the minority. This was a particularly difficult challenge as they sought to find common ground on the terrain of religion.

The Founding Fathers believed that a successful republic required a virtuous people. That meant expressions of faith must be encouraged. Yet the Founders also rightly worried about the religious persecution that too often accompanied an official state religion. Indeed, many of the early colonists in the New World were religious refugees. How could they resolve this conflict?

The answer was to protect the right of the people to express their faith while restricting—indeed, forbidding—the government's right to establish a national religion.

In this way, the American nation, unique among nations at the time, chose to make religion the business of the people, not of the government's. Because of this, individual Americans freely, openly, and repeatedly expressed their faith in the public square. Perhaps the best example of this willingness for an individual American to assert his faith in a public arena occurred at George Washington's inauguration. After reciting the oath of office, Washington, without prompting from anyone, voluntarily added the words "So help me, God." In doing so, he established the first of many precedents he would set as president. More than two hundred years later, forty-three presidents have now completed their oath of office with these very words that are not part of the oath, but are very much a part of the American tradition.

Some might object that this violates the "separation of church and state." But what Washington practiced at his inauguration and what Jefferson explained to the Danbury Baptists is that no wall exists preventing Americans from expressing their faith openly. Indeed, the First Amendment specifically protects the right to religious expression. No, the wall is simply to protect people of faith from government interference in their religious practices.

<>

As America begins a new century, our faith continues to serve us well, just as it has for more than two hundred years. Still, there are those who would like to teach our children that faith is a private matter that should never enter the public square. Not only is this not constitutional, it's not healthy for the American republic. Like iron is sharpened by iron, the more voices that are heard in the public square the stronger our public discourse will be. America needs the involvement of all its citizens, not just some and that certainly includes people of faith. By getting involved, by speaking out, by taking action, people of faith aren't violating the First Amendment; they are validating it.

People of faith have written glorious chapters in the story of America. Many of the great social movements in American history have been inspired and led by people of faith, including the greatest of them all: the civil rights movement. Take Dr. Martin Luther King, Jr., a Baptist minister who used his faith to help change America and the world. His voice joined in the great chorus of American debate and his persuasion led to better policies and a better nation. King's leadership proved once again that we are a stronger nation when people of faith are encouraged to speak out and step up.

King is one of many Americans through history who reminded us again of the simple truth that guided our Founding Fathers: freedom of religion, not freedom from religion.

SECTION THREE

THE PURSUIT
OF HAPPINESS

CHAPTER NINE

WE VALUE RESPONSIBILITY

"If any blame or fault attaches to the attempt, it is mine alone."

—Dwight Eisenhower, June 1944

THE MOMENT OF DECISION had arrived. As the men gathered in the room, smartly dressed in their pressed uniforms, they watched as their leader paced the floor. And paced. And paced.

This was England's Southwick House on June 5, 1944. Here, the leaders of the Supreme Headquarters, Allied Expeditionary Force met on the eve of the single greatest decision of World War II. Would they go forward with the planned D-Day invasion? They all had an opinion, but only one had the responsibility. And so he paced.

◇

It was an unlikely journey that brought General Dwight David Eisenhower to this moment. A relatively obscure career military officer, Eisenhower had never commanded troops in battle. Against his wishes, he spent World War I behind a desk in Washington. In the years leading to the outbreak of World War II, he quietly, steadily rose in the ranks. All the while he established a reputation as an original thinker, a good manager, and a compelling leader. When Japan attacked Pearl Harbor, he was asked to create a plan for the defense of the Pacific. He did. He accomplished that task so well that he soon found himself in charge of American troops in the European Theater.

Things didn't go so well at first. In his very first battle against the Germans, Eisenhower's inexperienced Americans were routed at Kasserine Pass in North Africa. Yet Eisenhower, like all great leaders, still saw the mountaintops from this valley of defeat. He told the officials in Washington that the combat experience would teach his soldiers important lessons and make them "battle wise." He was right.

Soon, Eisenhower's troops were teaching the Germans a few lessons on the battlefield. After the Allies successfully retook North Africa and Sicily, it was time to think about re-taking the continent of Europe. It was time for D-Day.

◇

For two years, Eisenhower had waited for this moment. Now at last, the Allied troops were strong and ready to launch an amphibious invasion of the European mainland. The risk was great and so were the stakes. Nothing less than an invasion of Europe could lead to the demise of Hitler's reign.

If he pulled off the invasion, Eisenhower would be the first man in nearly a thousand years to lead a successful military assault across the English Channel. If he failed, Hitler would be stronger than ever. The war, in all likelihood, would be lost.

And so it was that Eisenhower came to pace the floor at Southwick House. The invasion force had been ready for a couple of days, but the weather was unwilling. Now the weather cooperated, promising to give the Allies a thirty-six-hour window in which to launch an attack. Eisenhower had given a preliminary go-ahead the previous day. It was not too late to pull the troops back again. But it was time to make a decision.

As the general walked the floor at the British estate that fateful day, he stopped, paused, and then spoke. "O.K.," he said, "let's go."

Instantly, cheers erupted in the room as the various generals and admirals voiced their approval. Within hours, America and its allies would finally take the fight to the Nazis in Europe. Within minutes, Eisenhower, Supreme Allied Commander, went from the most powerful commander in the war to a virtual spectator. Having given the order, he now relied on his troops to follow it. As far as the invasion was concerned, his work was done. Theirs was just beginning.

Yet Eisenhower carried out an additional duty that day. After visiting some of the troops before they left on their mission, Eisenhower returned to the grounds of Southwick House. Here, he took a moment to reflect. Then he took responsibility for a lost battle that had yet to be fought.

Taking a pen and a pad of paper, Eisenhower wrote a press release to give to reporters in the event the attack failed:

"Our landings in the Cherbourg-Havre area have failed to gain a satisfactory foothold, and I have withdrawn the troops. My decision to attack [at Normandy] at this time and place was based upon the best information available. The troops, the air and Navy did all that Bravery and devotion to duty could do. If any blame or fault attaches to the attempt, it is mine alone."

Eisenhower then put the paper in his wallet, ventured to dinner, and waited to hear if events would require the release of this statement.

<>

Many people are able to take responsibility for their own actions. But how many people would take responsibility for the actions of others? Eisenhower's greatness was found not just in his ability to organize an invasion, but in his willingness to accept the blame for its failure. In this, Eisenhower was acting as a good general and a good American.

Americans have always understood that our freedom is a two-sided coin. On one side, the rights we enjoy. And the other side, the responsibilities we bear. We hear much about the rights of Americans. But we seldom hear enough about the responsibilities that come with them.

Yet for America to be great, Americans must do great things. Nothing is greater or more powerful than when an individual American steps forward, speaks out, or stands up for what is right. This is the essence of responsibility and the duty of every American.

◇

When I was growing up, a popular song challenged listeners: "Oh, people look at you and me. Are we too blind to see, do we simply turn our heads and look the other way as the world turns."

Today, many people in our society don't just look the other way; they don't look at all. Too many times too many Americans are unaware of their responsibilities—to themselves, their families, their communities, and their nation.

The history of America tells the story of people who accepted their responsibilities and treated them as opportunities toward making a difference. Rather than a burden, Americans have traditionally seen responsibility as a blessing, one that blesses their own lives and the lives of those around them.

So what is responsibility? Perhaps the best definition can be found at the United States Holocaust Memorial Museum in Washington where visitors learn about the horrors of concentration camps and gas chambers. They also learn how mankind can prevent such a horrific tragedy from reoccurring.

A simple phrase can be seen at the museum: "Thou shalt not be a victim. Thou salt not be a perpetrator. Above all, thou salt not be a bystander."

At this museum, the true meaning of responsibility in all its applications can be seen.

First, we are not "victims." Responsibility means taking charge of your life. No bad situation or unfortunate circumstances are responsible for what occurs in your life. You are.

Taking responsibility means parents remembering their most important job is raising their children. It means working hard and living right. It means sharing the credit with others when things go right and taking the blame yourself if things go wrong. Above all, it means knowing that you and you alone are responsible for your actions. If you have a job, do it and do it well. If you have a family, love them and provide for them. If you have a dream, pursue it and don't give up. You are the master of your own destiny. Don't be victimized. Be victorious.

Second, the Holocaust Memorial Museum urges citizens not to be "perpetrators." Obviously, being responsible means doing what is legal, what is ethical, and what is right. Beyond that, being responsible also means being a part of the solution, not the problem. Rather than creating challenges for those around you, help those around you meet their challenges. Promote goodwill in your neighborhood by performing good acts. Too often Americans lash out at others rather than fostering a climate of mutual understanding and goodwill. In a society lacking in personal responsibility, we see neighbor suing neighbor, and friend attacking friend. Both the individual and the community are better served when people aren't perpetrators, but partners.

Finally, the Holocaust Memorial Museum defines responsibility as refusing to be a "bystander." We have all seen examples of people who are bystanders, spectators, and observers. When it comes to the important challenges our nation faces, these bystanders claim they know nothing and won't do anything. Perhaps the best example occurs on Election Day when half of all American voters become bystanders by staying home and not voting.

The good news is more Americans are accepting the important challenge of responsibility in the wake of September 11. Voter registration is up and public awareness about current events (especially the War on Terror) is high. These vital signs show America's sense of responsibility is healthy. But it can be even healthier.

First, organize your life. Get on top of it before it gets on top of you. Take care of school, work, and family commitments. Second, accept responsibility for those around you. Be a peacemaker and not a troublemaker. Look for ways to help those in need. By helping others, you are really helping yourself. Finally, don't be a bystander. When you are eighteen, register for selective service and register to vote. Do your duty to your country. Keep informed about issues. Always look for ways to be involved.

In the end, responsibility becomes less of a burden and more of a blessing. By taking charge of your decisions and your life, by helping those around you, and by being involved in your nation, you will find great inspiration. In giving, we always end up receiving much more.

So accept responsibility for your life, your community, and your nation.

CHAPTER TEN

WE VALUE PROGRESS

"The single thing which makes any man happiest is the realization that he has worked up to the limits of his ability, his capacity."

—Neil Armstrong, 1969

IN JULY, 1969, America stood at a crossroads. Hundreds of thousands of troops were fighting and dying in Vietnam. More people were waging protests at home. College campuses were finally quiet after an angry spring of sit-ins and demonstrations. But the race riots of 1968 were still a smoldering memory.

Yet out of these dark days came a shining moment. On July 20, 1969, three men stepped into an aircraft and into history.

On that hot summer day, Neil Armstrong, Buzz Aldrin, and Michael Collins were on their way to the moon. If they succeeded, they would complete the greatest feat in the history of exploration. Yet the odds were against them. They were attempting to do the impossible.

Armstrong himself thought the odds of coming back alive were fifty-fifty. Michael Collins feared the vessel would "blow up." While few Americans knew what to expect as the flight embarked, even fewer knew about the events leading to this momentous event.

The journey to the moon may have taken off from Cape Kennedy that July, but it began in 1957. And while the journey was based on science, politics launched it.

◇

On October 4, 1957, the Soviet Union shocked the world when it successfully launched the first man-made satellite into space. The artificial device, called "Sputnik I," was not terribly important as a military weapon, but as propaganda, it was a smash hit, launching the start of the space age.

Across the world, people talked about the Soviets's ability to beat the Americans in space. In the United States, people worried about the Soviets not only dominating Eastern Europe but all of space.

In Washington, Senator John F. Kennedy accused the Republican White House of allowing a "missile gap" to develop between America and the Soviets. In the press, one scientist called Sputnik a worse setback for America than Pearl Harbor.

At the White House, Eisenhower, the former general who was now president, urged calm. What Eisenhower couldn't say publicly is that his intelligence services were keeping a close watch on the Soviets. He knew that Sputnik was a public relations success, but he also knew that the satellite did not contain military or scientific equipment. He assured Americans that Sputnik did not worry him "one iota."

But Americans were uncertain. If the Soviets were able to put a satellite into space before America, what else could they do?

One year later, Congress passed legislation creating the National Aeronautical and Space Agency, and Eisenhower signed it. The Cold War had been expanded. And the United States and Soviet Union space race began.

◇

By 1962, John Kennedy switched his title from "senator" to "president." But his concern about space followed him to the Oval Office. To raise the stakes and galvanize the nation, Kennedy decided to propose a bold national goal. He urged the nation to "put a man on the moon" before the end of the decade.

In making his case for the project, Kennedy specifically compared it to the efforts to climb Mount Everest. He quoted one of the mountains' explorers, saying he wanted to climb the mountain "because it is there." So, too, Kennedy argued, was the moon. He knew that America gained new strength when it accepted new challenges.

With that in mind, one of the greatest collective efforts in American history began in earnest. For nearly a decade, more than 400,000 people worked at various places—the National Aeronautics and Space Administration, university labs, and military installations—with one goal: to put a man on the moon.

Along the way, these scientists designed cutting-edge technologies and innovative equipment to help make a lunar landing possible. Not only would these inventions make such a feat possible, they would eventually make life on earth better. Even today, we experience innovations that were originally created by NASA: X-Rays in hospitals. Laser angioplasty for heart patients. Portable computers. Solar energy technology. Even ski boots. NASA was creative because they were attempting the impossible.

At times, it looked as if getting to the moon would be more than impossible. In 1967, three astronauts died when their Apollo I capsule caught fire on the launch pad. Some wondered if the space race was worth it. Still, the scientists and the astronauts kept pushing forward. The mission was important. They weren't just out to beat the Soviets; they were out to make America better.

And perhaps no one believed this more than the man chosen to lead the trip to the moon.

<>

Rarely has history so perfectly matched the man, the mission, and the moment. Neil Armstrong was destined to walk on the moon. As a young man, he dreamed of flying. In fact, he earned his pilot's license before he received his driver's license.

He flew seventy-eight combat missions in Korea as a naval aviator. In 1962, he became a test pilot for NASA. Whether he knew it or not, he was building an impressive resume that would be hard to ignore once NASA was ready to go to the moon.

More than his pedigree, Armstrong's sense of purpose resounded. He believed in being the best. He believed in making the most out of every situation. As he once told a reporter: "The single thing which makes any man happiest is the realization that he has worked up to the limits of his ability, his capacity…It's all the better, of course, if this work has contributed to knowledge, or toward moving the human race a little farther forward."

As a trained engineer and pilot, Armstrong saw the work NASA did for preparation in the moon adventure. He knew that the developing technologies would do more than take him into outer space; they would change the lives of American citizens.

Nevertheless, Armstrong, a realist, knew that he might not survive the trip to the moon. But the future belongs to the brave. Like so many other Americans of his generation, Armstrong believed space was indeed the next frontier, the last great chance for exploration.

As Apollo 11 crossed the sky toward the moon, Armstrong looked out at space and pondered the moment when the lunar module would land safely so that he would set foot on the moon. Set foot on the moon! He almost couldn't believe it himself. If all went well, he would be the first man to walk on the moon.

Such a big event. Such a huge achievement. He struggled to put it into words. He thought about what he wanted to say if and when his feet touched down on the moon. He kept thinking about how it was a nice moment for him personally, but it was a colossal moment for the world. This event wasn't about one person, it was about every person. So he formulated a phrase that he thought perfectly captured the moment. When he landed on the moon, he would say: "That's one small step for a man, one giant leap for mankind."

On July 20, the lunar module landed. Armstrong prepared to dismount, along with Aldrin. Hundreds of millions of people around the word sat glued to their television sets, watching in disbelief as Armstrong stepped out of the capsule. He put his foot down and made history. He remembered to speak the words but he was so overwhelmed by the moment that he flubbed them. He left out the word "a," and thus said that "it was a small step for man and a giant leap for mankind." Like all memorable quotes, the meaning was obvious. People understood. And the line, like the trip itself, was immortalized.

The return trip was successful and safe. The three astronauts received awards and parades. And today, decades later, it is still amazing to say it—these brave men walked on the moon. After that, America ventured to the moon several times. New plans are now being made for a trip to Mars. But who will ever forget that first journey to the moon? And what it meant for our nation and what it gave our lives.

<>

Progress is like rain. It showers blessings on everything. When Neil Armstrong and Buzz Aldrin landed on the moon, NASA achieved perhaps the greatest technological feat in history. Nothing else compares to it. Charles Lindbergh flew across the Atlantic. Sir Edmund Hillary reached the summit at Mount Everest. These, however, happened inside the confines of our own planet. Imagine venturing to another world. That's what America did in 1969.

The greatest blessings of the moon landing were perhaps felt by ordinary citizens on earth. Technology improved. Medical research improved. Quality of life improved. Because NASA was forced to meet a goal, it developed some amazing inventions along the way.

There is a lesson in all of this about the importance of goals. What if Kennedy hadn't challenged our country to put a man on the moon by the end of the decade? What if he had just suggested that we simply try and reach the moon? Chances are we wouldn't have made it.

What can we learn about goal-setting from this story?

First, goals must be specific. Anything else is hope, not a goal.

Second, goals must have a timeline. Having a schedule helps to focus.

Third, a plan must accompany them. NASA worked on a plan that culminated in Apollo 11's moon landing.

This is how progress is achieved. Setting a goal with a specific objective, creating a schedule, and following through with a plan. It works in science; it works in politics; it works in everyday life.

America has always been a nation of progress. We are always moving forward and upward, taking on new projects, exploring new territories. A few years ago, we explored the moon. Today, we explore the human genome. A few years ago, we solved the problems that prevented manned flights in space. Today, we are solving medical problems with new technologies in science labs throughout the country. A few years ago, we created the modern computer. Today, we are revolutionizing the Information Age with novel innovations in high-tech arenas.

There is always progress to be made because work always needs to be done. That's true for you, too. Whether at home or at school, set goals for yourself. Have a schedule. Make a plan. As Thomas Jefferson once said, "It's amazing what we can do when we are constantly doing."

CHAPTER ELEVEN

WE VALUE COURAGE

"A blessing in disguise."

—Eleanor Roosevelt

WHITE PUFFS OF CLOUDS and a golden sun punctuated the pale blue sky that August morning. Caressed by a gentle breeze, the day at Campobello, New Brunswick began the same as most of its summer days: bright, peaceful, warm, and glorious. In the nearby Harbor of Fundy, a ship named *Vireo* glided across the waters toward a nearby island. A vibrant, athletic thirty-nine-year-old was on board along with several of his children. After docking at the Island, the family put out a small fire they spotted in the branches of the evergreens. This work exhausted them. They were ready for a break. Entering the water, the family swam together before loading up the boat and heading back home.

When they arrived, the father complained that he was exhausted. He sat down, read the paper, and then went upstairs. He then got in bed and fell asleep. It was August 10, 1921. And it was the last time Franklin Delano Roosevelt would ever walk.

◇

On the political canvas of 1921, Roosevelt's colors were very bright, indeed. Blessed with a famous last name and an inherited fortune, he was capable of captivating large audiences with his speeches and charming individuals with his charisma. His resume was already sterling—Assistant Secretary of the Navy during World War I, a state senator, and in 1920, the Democratic Party's vice presidential candidate. Although his ticket lost the 1920 election, it did nothing to lessen his appeal. The defeat was blamed on the name at the top of the ticket, not his.

He traveled to his summer home for some rest that. During his vacation he undoubtedly considered his future. Would he run for president? Or should he first run for governor? These are not the decisions of ordinary politicians but rather the choices that face gifted and great men. And Roosevelt fit the bill.

Until tragedy struck. Before a vaccination was discovered in the 1950s, many Americans contracted polio. But Roosevelt was not just any American. He possessed big ambitions and even bigger dreams. Since the early 1900s, he had said that he planned to be president like his cousin and hero, Theodore Roosevelt. But that ambition was dead now.

Within days, doctors confirmed that Roosevelt was paralyzed from his waist downward. This gallant and graceful man would be confined to a life of immobility, pain, frustration, and disability. Having wealth, he could simply retire to his Hyde Park, New York home and collect stamps or read books. Surely a life of action was out of the question. Certainly, this man would have to readjust his aspirations.

But Roosevelt disagreed. Almost from the very beginning of the crisis, Roosevelt remained confident, calm, and above all, committed to pursuing his dreams no matter the cost and to walking again no matter the odds. Hindsight often obscures how remarkable this determination was. Decades before polio would be cured, Roosevelt was convinced he would once more move his legs and walk. He was convinced he could lead a normal life and that he should still be president one day.

Another amazing chapter in the American story began that August day in 1921. A story of courage, perseverance, and, ultimately, triumph. Only one man has ever been chosen as the leader of his nation despite being unable to walk in history. That man was Roosevelt.

But the road from the summer house to the White House was a long, tortured, and winding one. Roosevelt had to endure years of painful rehabilitation. Strategies to reassure voters of his capabilities had to be developed. And a way of walking had to be devised.

Historian Hugh Gregory Gallagher called this "FDR's Splendid Deception." Roosevelt began by committing himself to rehabilitation with painful and arduous exercises. Roosevelt soon established the Warm Springs Foundation in Georgia to provide other disabled Americans with a place to relax and rehabilitate. Indeed, twenty-four years after contracting polio, Roosevelt would spend his last moments not in the White House, but at his beloved retreat in Warm Springs.

Second, Roosevelt devised a strategy to hide his disability, not out of shame, but out of political necessity. The America of the 1920s and the 1930s was not ready to elect Americans with disabilities. Roosevelt had to be seen as vibrant and healthy. Photos of him in his wheelchair were avoided. Newsreel films showing him being pushed around in his chair were discouraged. In this strategy, he was remarkably successful. Today the Franklin D. Roosevelt Presidential Library and Museum houses 35,000 photos of Roosevelt. These cover his entire life; only two show him in a wheelchair.

The most important part of Roosevelt's effort to overcome his disability and run for president began with his determination to walk again. In fact, not only did Roosevelt believe he would walk; he refused to admit he couldn't. Years later, Eleanor Roosevelt would say of her husband that he had "never said he could not walk."

Actually, Roosevelt developed a way of walking. He discovered that he could lean on the arm of one of his aides and balance himself with a cane in the other arm. He would then use his muscular arms to move himself forward. One newsreel film exists showing Roosevelt walking in this fashion. To see this film is to witness courage, unadulterated and inspiring.

Roosevelt failed to see himself as a victim and refused to abandon his dreams. In 1932 he was elected president, followed by an unprecedented three reelections. During his presidency America emerged from the Great Depression and confronted two evil empires in German fascism and Japanese imperialism. He was a great American and a great president who achieved it all in spite of his paralysis.

Indeed, some might say that he achieved such greatness because of his paralysis. Historian Ted Morgan wrote that Roosevelt being in a wheelchair fundamentally changed how he worked. Before, he was an impatient man always in a hurry. As a state legislator, if he didn't like what one of his colleagues was saying during a meeting, he simply got up and walked away. Not so after 1921. Roosevelt now had to sit, and that meant he learned to listen. Even Eleanor Roosevelt once said that polio was a "blessing in disguise" to her husband because it gave him a sense of empathy with those less fortunate.

One thing is clear—Roosevelt met the challenge of polio with tremendous courage. At the height of World War II, Roosevelt's distant cousin and wartime ally, Winston Churchill, remarked that courage is the first of all the virtues because without it none of the others are possible. No one demonstrated this more compellingly or more often than Roosevelt. Getting out of bed in the morning was an act of courage. Running for president was an act of courage. It is no surprise that Roosevelt was so undaunted by the challenges that faced him as president. After polio, taking on the Nazis didn't seem so impossible.

Roosevelt's life can be seen as a mighty river, winding and struggling mightily to reach the sea of greatness. Undaunted by the challenges fate handed him, Roosevelt kept surging forward toward his goal. It was his glory that he made it. It was history's blessing that he did it so beautifully. For his was a great presidency that made the world more free and more secure. But his public achievements would not have happened without his extraordinary personal courage.

<>

Most of us will never have to face such extreme challenges like Roosevelt did. Few of us will ever have to take the test of courage that faces young American troops in places like Baghdad and Kabul. But all of us will struggle in our own way with our own battles. Every life is a series of choices. The poet Robert Frost famously wrote about this choice when he spoke of his pride in having chosen the "the road less traveled" and that it made all the difference. Years earlier, another American literary giant, Ralph Waldo Emerson, encouraged his readers to pass up the well-trodden path and instead go where no one else has been and "blaze a trail."

Every person faces this dilemma. Do what's easy or what's hard? Take the easy road or the difficult path? Historically, Americans have always had the courage to make the hard choices. George Washington was a wealthy planter with everything to lose by fighting against the British and yet he did. Harriet Tubman, a runaway slave, didn't have to risk her life by helping to free other slaves but she did. Dr. Martin Luther King, Jr. talked about the death threats against him and said he wasn't eager to become a martyr but he did.

Americans are nothing if not courageous. But courage is not limited to famous Americans. Every time an American risks his savings to start a new business, we see courage. Every time an American enlists in the military, we see courage. Every time an American volunteers to minister to inmates, we see courage. And every time an American confronts a disease, we see courage.

Roosevelt reminds us that our greatest challenges are sometimes our greatest blessings. Each obstacle overcome, each battle won, each issue confronted builds character. We need challenges to grow. We need tough choices to test our character. But you don't have to be a soldier or a famous American to have courage. Make an effort to do the courageous thing. Volunteer at a prison. Consider serving in the military. Have the courage to resist your peers. Be brave and stay away from drugs. Go your own way and be your own person. Most importantly, choose to make the hard choices in your everyday life. Choose courage and it will make all the difference.

CHAPTER TWELVE

WE VALUE VISION

"You can be sick and get to the top..."

—Dr. Antonia Novello

"**B**UT I KNOW, SOMEHOW," Martin Luther King, Jr. once said, "that only when it is dark enough, can you see the stars." Life has a way of giving us both highs and lows. And many times, a dark moment can lead directly to a bright shining one. Many times, out of darkness comes vision.

Antonia Coello is a woman who personifies vision. She was born in the Puerto Rican town of Fajardo during the days of World War II. Yet from birth, she had her own battle to fight. A colon abnormality would plague for years until surgery freed her from the pain. She was "lost in the system," she later remembered. And she had to wait years before she received the proper treatment.

So often in life, tragedy often gives way to triumph. Indeed, one can often spark the other. Young Antonia's health issues inspired her to seek a medical career.

After she was cured at the Mayo Clinic, she was healthy and eager to heal the illnesses of others. After falling in love and marrying Joseph Novello she devoted herself to studying medicine so she could treat people who suffered as she had. She had come a long way from the sick little girl she had once been.

She had always had the vision to help others. Now her vision broadened even more. Not too long after her medical career began, she decided that she wanted to do even more to help the sick. Public service seemed like another way to help even more people. She began working at the National Institutes of Health just outside of Washington, DC.

Her vision and hard work had now led her into government service. But it was about to take her even farther. She eventually served as Deputy Director of the National Institute of Child Health and Human Development. Though she was now one of the most powerful women in medicine, she never forgot who she was, as well as who she used to be. She remembered being a little girl in Puerto Rico in need of treatment.

Perhaps this led her to pay close attention to the issue of pediatric AIDS. In the late 1980s, AIDS was still a largely taboo subject. Like the lepers of the Bible times, most people preferred that AIDS patients not be seen or heard. It was not only a disease without a cure, it was a disease with a stigma.

People like Dr. Novello helped change that. As a doctor, she knew that her first job was to treat the patient. As a public servant, she served others, especially the sick, the vulnerable, and the young. "I was one of those kids that got lost in the system of health," she once said. "I was supposed to have surgery when I was eight, and I didn't have surgery until I was eighteen. So, when you get lost in the track of medicine, then you want to be somebody that will solve the problems for others. And I think that motivation was there all my life."

And so she did what she had always done since was a little girl—she showed vision. At a time when AIDS wasn't talked about, she talked about it. And people started listening. Soon, even the White House listened. It was 1990 and the nation needed a new Surgeon General of the United States. The White House "needed someone who knew AIDS," Dr. Novello later said. And so President George Bush swore in as the nation's top doctor a little girl who had grown up in Puerto Rico. "Mr. President," she said after she was sworn in, "thank you very much for bringing the West Side Story to the West Wing." She was the first woman and the first Hispanic to hold the prestigious job of Surgeon General.

While she served in that role for three years, Dr. Novello continued to speak out about AIDS and stand up for public health. She went all around the country promoting health. And later, as the Special Representative for Health and Nutrition for UNICEF, she took her message all over the world.

Still, she never forgot her roots. She never who she was and how far she had come. "I was one of those children who were sick when they were born," she said years later. "So, all my life, I spent two weeks every summer in the hospital. So, the people that I learned to relate to since I was little were doctors and nurses....I always felt I was going to be a doctor."

Even now, people remember her work as Surgeon General and her inspiring rise from being the patient to being the doctor. "To this day, when I go to Puerto Rico and I walk down the street, grandmothers stop and hug me, they kiss me, they thank me, and they say, 'I want my granddaughter to be like you.'"

Ultimately, her story is a testament to the power of vision. As she puts it, "you can be sick and get to the top...." By having the vision to picture herself as a doctor, by having the vision of helping others like she had been helped, and by having the vision to use her own suffering to help alleviate the suffering of others, Dr. Novello made a difference for her patients and her country.

<>

Vision is what guides us through our dark times. By seeing how things ought to be, we can often overcome the way things are. By focusing on what lies ahead, we can move beyond where we are.

America exists today because the Founding Fathers had the vision to see beyond their troubles to a bright future. They saw their challenge as an opportunity; they saw their dark times as the last few moments before a new dawn would break.

Their vision was one of a truly democratic nation, where the people, not a sovereign, governed. Their vision was one of freedom: the freedom to earn a living, raise a family, and yes, make a difference. Their vision was one of a country at peace with itself and the world.

Just think how different the world would be today if they have fallen victim to their fears instead of their dreams; if they had accepted the *status quo* instead of creating a new world based on their vision.

Every one of us needs vision. We need a vision for ourselves and our future. We need a vision for our communities and our country.

How do we create our own vision?

Like Dr. Novello, the key is to start with you. What is your story? What are your experiences? How can you use the road you've traveled to help the journey of someone else? Dr. Novello was a sick child and decided to devote herself to helping other sick kids. She decided to turn her nightmare into a dream.

By grounding your vision in your own experience, you bring a certain expertise with you. By dealing with the illnesses of children, Dr. Novello wasn't just talking about a subject she had studied, but a condition through which she had lived. Her story gave her perspective, which is another way to say vision.

Once you have looked at your own life and determined how you can best use your story, make sure your vision is focused outwardly.

Sargent Shriver was John F. Kennedy's brother-in-law and has devoted his life to causes like the Special Olympics. He once said that in order to serve others, you must first do away with your mirrors. Only when the mirrors are gone can you focus on someone other than yourself.

Having a vision means seeing others. It means serving others. It means helping others. Yes, it's important to have a dream. But the dream must be deeply rooted in helping others. A vision must look outward, not inward. It must be about something bigger than yourself.

WE VALUE VISION

Every successful journey has a vision. Every plane has a flight plan; every ship has a course to chart. So it is with life.

It's never too early or too late to develop a vision. Base it on who you are. But devote it to serving others. Turn your struggle into someone else's blessing. Make your journey one where the destination is serving others. Put away your mirror and focus on others. That's a vision that will bless you and all those around you.

CONCLUSION
THE VALUE OF VALUES

THROUGHOUT THE WORLD, their job is the most difficult and the most rewarding. They face enormous challenges. The work they perform never ends. And the consequences of their actions are far reaching. For them, there will be no clocking out at the end of the day, and there is seldom overtime or extra pay. Their reward, however, can never be measured by dollars or cents.

Yet they are professionals in every sense: competent and committed, skillful and successful. Every day in every way, these professionals are called upon to do it all: To provide a soothing word of encouragement to lift spirits, to teach skills, to impart values, to transform children into adults.

Who are these miracle workers? Why would they agree to do the impossible? They are parents, teachers, coaches, and mentors. And theirs is a labor of love. They do their jobs because they love children and want the best for them.

To teach and raise kids today, people need help. In a small way, this book is way to help, too. It serves as a guide for helping parents and teachers show children the greatness that can be found in the goodness of America.

Is America perfect? No. Is she always right? Not at all. Are there sad chapters that could also have been written in this book? Sure. But the whole of the American story is a good one and it deserves to be told, to be taught, and to be learned.

First lady Laura Bush once famously said that before she and her husband had any kids they had a couple of theories. A few years later, they had a couple of kids and no more theories. This book is not about theories on education. It's about shared values. Simple, straightforward, and solid principles that have made America great for two hundred years and will help make a difference in the lives of your students.

It was President Ronald Reagan who reminded us that America is a shining city on a hill. It's time to remind our children of that, too. Show them. Teach them. And build a greater America of the future in your classroom today.

From George Washington to Abraham Lincoln, from Neil Armstrong to Dr. Martin Luther King, Jr. the heroes in this book are alive to us today, pointing the way, guiding us into the 21st century. Life, liberty, and the pursuit of happiness. More than just words on paper, they serve as the values of America. Our children deserve to know them. Today, and always.

Thanks for teaching, raising, and loving your kids. And thanks for sharing America's values with America's children.

APPENDICES:

HISTORICAL DOCUMENTS CITED

APPENDIX A
THE DECLARATION OF INDEPENDENCE

The unanimous Declaration of the thirteen united States of America,

When in the course of human events, it becomes necessary for one People to dissolve the Political Bands which have connected them with another, and to assume among the Powers of the Earth, the separate and equal Station to which the Laws of Nature and of Nature's God entitle them, a decent Respect to the Opinions of Mankind requires that they should declare the causes which impel them to the Separation.

WE hold these Truths to be self-evident, that all Men are created equal, that they are endowed by their Creator with certain unalienable Rights, that among these are Life, Liberty and the Pursuit of Happiness—That to secure these Rights, Governments are instituted among Men, deriving their just Powers from the Consent of the Governed, that whenever any Form of Government becomes destructive of these Ends, it is the Right of the People to alter or to abolish it, and to institute new Government, laying its Foundation on such Principles, and organizing its Powers in such Form, as to them shall seem most likely to effect their Safety and Happiness. Prudence, indeed, will dictate that Governments long established should not be changed for light and transient Causes; and accordingly all Experience hath shewn, that Mankind are more disposed to suffer, while Evils are sufferable, than to right themselves by abolishing the Forms to which they are accustomed. But when a long Train of Abuses and Usurpations, pursuing invariably the same Object, evinces a Design to reduce them under absolute Despotism, it is their Right, it is their Duty, to throw off such Government, and to provide new Guards for their future Security. Such has been the patient Sufferance of these Colonies; and such is now the Necessity which constrains them to alter their former Systems of Government. The History of the present King of Great-Britain is a History of repeated Injuries and Usurpations, all having in direct Ob-

ject the Establishment of an absolute Tyranny over these States. To prove this, let Facts be submitted to a candid World.

HE has refused his Assent to Laws, the most wholesome and necessary for the public Good.

HE has forbidden his Governors to pass Laws of immediate and pressing Importance, unless suspended in their Operation till his Assent should be obtained; and when so suspended, he has utterly neglected to attend to them

HE has refused to pass other Laws for the Accommodation of large Districts of People, unless those People would relinquish the Right of Representation in the Legislature, a Right inestimable to them, and formidable to Tyrants only.

HE has called together Legislative Bodies at Places unusual, uncomfortable, and distant from the Depository of their public Records, for the sole Purpose of fatiguing them into Compliance with his Measures.

HE has dissolved Representative Houses repeatedly, for opposing with manly Firmness his Invasions on the Rights of the People.

HE has refused for a long Time, after such Dissolutions, to cause others to be elected; whereby the Legislative Powers, incapable of the Annihilation, have returned to the People at large for their exercise; the State remaining in the mean time exposed to all the Dangers of Invasion from without, and the Convulsions within.

HE has endeavoured to prevent the Population of these States; for that Purpose obstructing the Laws for Naturalization of Foreigners; refusing to pass others to encourage their Migrations hither, and raising the Conditions of new Appropriations of Lands.

HE has obstructed the Administration of Justice, by refusing his Assent to Laws for establishing Judiciary Powers

HE has made Judges dependent on his Will alone, for the Tenure of their Offices, and the Amount and Payment of their Salaries.

HE has erected a Multitude of new Offices, and sent hither Swarms of Officers to harrass our People, and eat out their Substance.

HE has kept among us, in Times of Peace, Standing Armies, without the consent of our Legislatures.

HE has affected to render the Military independent of and superior to the Civil Power.

HE has combined with others to subject us to a Jurisdiction foreign to our Constitution, and unacknowledged by our Laws; giving his Assent to their Acts of pretended Legislation:

FOR quartering large Bodies of Armed Troops among us;

FOR protecting them, by a mock Trial, from Punishment for any Murders which they should commit on the Inhabitants of these States:

FOR cutting off our Trade with all Parts of the World:

FOR imposing Taxes on us without our Consent:

FOR depriving us, in many Cases, of the Benefits of Trial by Jury:

FOR transporting us beyond Seas to be tried for pretended Offences:

FOR abolishing the free System of English Laws in a neighbouring Province, establishing therein an arbitrary Government, and enlarging its Boundaries, so as to render it at once an Example and fit Instrument for introducing the same absolute Rules into these Colonies:

FOR taking away our Charters, abolishing our most valuable Laws, and altering fundamentally the Forms of our Governments:

FOR suspending our own Legislatures, and declaring themselves invested with Power to legislate for us in all Cases whatsoever.

HE has abdicated Government here, by declaring us out of his Protection and waging War against us.

HE has plundered our Seas, ravaged our Coasts, burnt our Towns, and destroyed the Lives of our People.

HE is, at this Time, transporting large Armies of foreign Mercenaries to compleat the Works of Death, Desolation, and Tyranny, already begun with circumstances of Cruelty and Perfidy, scarcely paralleled in the most barbarous Ages, and totally unworthy the Head of a civilized Nation.

HE has constrained our fellow Citizens taken Captive on the high Seas to bear Arms against their Country, to become the Executioners of their Friends and Brethren, or to fall themselves by their Hands.

HE has excited domestic Insurrections amongst us, and has endeavoured to bring on the Inhabitants of our Frontiers, the merciless

Indian Savages, whose known Rule of Warfare, is an undistinguished Destruction, of all Ages, Sexes and Conditions.

IN every stage of these Oppressions we have Petitioned for Redress in the most humble Terms: Our repeated Petitions have been answered only by repeated Injury. A Prince, whose Character is thus marked by every act which may define a Tyrant, is unfit to be the Ruler of a free People.

NOR have we been wanting in Attentions to our British Brethren. We have warned them from Time to Time of Attempts by their Legislature to extend an unwarrantable Jurisdiction over us. We have reminded them of the Circumstances of our Emigration and Settlement here. We have appealed to their native Justice and Magnanimity, and we have conjured them by the Ties of our common Kindred to disavow these Usurpations, which, would inevitably interrupt our Connections and Correspondence. They too have been deaf to the Voice of Justice and of Consanguinity. We must, therefore, acquiesce in the Necessity, which denounces our Separation, and hold them, as we hold the rest of Mankind, Enemies in War, in Peace, Friends.

WE, therefore, the Representatives of the UNITED STATES OF AMERICA, in GENERAL CONGRESS, Assembled, appealing to the Supreme Judge of the World for the Rectitude of our Intentions, do, in the Name, and by Authority of the good People of these Colonies, solemnly Publish and Declare, That these United Colonies are, and of Right ought to be, FREE AND INDEPENDENT STATES; that they are absolved from all Allegiance to the British Crown, and that all political Connection between them and the State of Great-Britain, is and ought to be totally dissolved; and that as FREE AND INDEPENDENT STATES, they have full Power to levy War, conclude Peace, contract Alliances, establish Commerce, and to do all other Acts and Things which INDEPENDENT STATES may of right do. And for the support of this Declaration, with a firm Reliance on the Protection of divine Providence, we mutually pledge to each other our Lives, our Fortunes, and our sacred Honor.

APPENDIX B
DR. MARTIN LUTHER KING, JR.'S "LETTER FROM BIRMINGHAM JAIL"

April 16, 1963

MY DEAR FELLOW CLERGYMEN:

While confined here in the Birmingham city jail, I came across your recent statement calling my present activities "unwise and untimely." Seldom do I pause to answer criticism of my work and ideas. If I sought to answer all the criticisms that cross my desk, my secretaries would have little time for anything other than such correspondence in the course of the day, and I would have no time for constructive work. But since I feel that you are men of genuine good will and that your criticisms are sincerely set forth, I want to try to answer your statements in what I hope will be patient and reasonable terms.

I think I should indicate why I am here. In Birmingham, since you have been influenced by the view which argues against "outsiders coming in." I have the honor of serving as president of the Southern Christian Leadership Conference, an organization operating in every southern state, with headquarters in Atlanta, Georgia. We have some eighty-five affiliated organizations across the South, and one of them is the Alabama Christian Movement for Human Rights. Frequently we share staff, educational and financial resources with our affiliates. Several months ago the affiliate here in Birmingham asked us to be on call to engage in a nonviolent direct-action program if such were deemed necessary. We readily consented, and when the hour came we lived up to our promise. So I, along with several members of my staff, am here because I was invited here I am here because I have organizational ties here.

But more basically, I am in Birmingham because injustice is here. Just as the prophets of the eighth century B.C. left their villages and carried their "thus saith the Lord" far beyond the boundaries of their home towns, and just as the Apostle Paul left his village of Tarsus and carried the gospel of Jesus Christ to the far corners of the Greco-Roman world, so am I. compelled to carry the gospel of freedom beyond my own home town. Like Paul, I must constantly respond to the Macedonian call for aid.

Moreover, I am cognizant of the interrelatedness of all communities and states. I cannot sit idly by in Atlanta and not be concerned about what happens in Birmingham. Injustice anywhere is a threat to justice everywhere. We are caught in an inescapable network of mutuality, tied in a single garment of destiny. Whatever affects one directly, affects all indirectly. Never again can we afford to live with the narrow, provincial "outside agitator" idea. Anyone who lives inside the United States can never be considered an outsider anywhere within its bounds.

You deplore the demonstrations taking place in Birmingham. But your statement, I am sorry to say, fails to express a similar concern for the conditions that brought about the demonstrations. I am sure that none of you would want to rest content with the superficial kind of social analysis that deals merely with effects and does not grapple with underlying causes. It is unfortunate that demonstrations are taking place in Birmingham, but it is even more unfortunate that the city's white power structure left the Negro community with no alternative.

In any nonviolent campaign there are four basic steps: collection of the facts to determine whether injustices exist; negotiation; self-purification; and direct action. We have gone through these steps in Birmingham. There can be no gainsaying the fact that racial injustice engulfs this community. Birmingham is probably the most thoroughly segregated city in the United States. Its ugly record of brutality is widely known. Negroes have experienced grossly unjust treatment in the courts. There have been more unsolved bombings of Negro homes and churches in Birmingham than in any other city in the nation.

These are the hard, brutal facts of the case. On the basis of these conditions, Negro leaders sought to negotiate with the city fathers. But the latter consistently refused to engage in good-faith negotiation.

Then, last September, came the opportunity to talk with leaders of Birmingham's economic community. In the course of the negotiations, certain promises were made by the merchants—for example, to remove the stores' humiliating racial signs. On the basis of these promises, the Reverend Fred Shuttlesworth and the leaders of the Alabama Christian Movement for Human Rights agreed to a moratorium on all demonstrations. As the weeks and months went by, we realized that we were the victims of a broken promise. A few signs, briefly removed, returned; the others remained.

As in so many past experiences, our hopes had been blasted, and the shadow of deep disappointment settled upon us. We had no alternative except to prepare for direct action, whereby we would present our very bodies as a means of laying our case before the conscience of the local and the national community. Mindful of the difficulties involved, we decided to undertake a process of self-purification. We began a series of workshops on nonviolence, and we repeatedly asked ourselves: "Are you able to accept blows without retaliating?" "Are you able to endure the ordeal of jail?" We decided to schedule our direct-action program for the Easter season, realizing that except for Christmas, this is the main shopping period of the year. Knowing that a strong economic-withdrawal program would be the by-product of direct action, we felt that this would be the best time to bring pressure to bear on the merchants for the needed change.

Then it occurred to us that Birmingham mayoralty election was coming up in March, and we speedily decided to postpone action until after election day. When we discovered that the Commissioner of Public Safety, Eugene "Bull" Connor, had piled up enough votes to be in the run-oat we decided again to postpone action until the day after the run-off so that the demonstrations could not be used to cloud the issues. Like many others, we waited to see Mr. Connor defeated, and to this end we endured postponement after postponement. Having aided in this community need, we felt that our direct-action program could be delayed no longer.

You may well ask: "Why direct action? Why sit-ins, marches and so forth? Isn't negotiation a better path?" You are quite right in calling for negotiation. Indeed, this is the very purpose of direct action. Nonviolent direct action seeks to create such a crisis and foster such a tension that a community which has constantly refused to negotiate is forced to confront the issue. It seeks so to dramatize the issue that it can no longer be ignored. My citing the creation of tension as part of the work of the non-violent-resister may sound rather shocking. But I must confess that I am not afraid of the word "tension." I have earnestly op-posed violent tension, but there is a type of constructive, non-violent tension which is necessary for growth. Just as Socrates felt that it was necessary to create a tension in the mind so that individuals could rise from the bondage of myths and half-truths to the unfettered realm of creative analysis and objective appraisal, so must we see the need for nonviolent gadflies to create the kind of tension in society that will help men rise from the dark depths of prejudice and racism to the majestic heights of understanding and brotherhood.

The purpose of our direct-action program is to create a situation so crisis-packed that it will inevitably open the door to negotiation. I therefore concur with you in your call for negotia-tion. Too long has our beloved Southland been bogged down in a tragic effort to live in monologue rather than dialogue.

One of the basic points in your statement is that the action that I and my associates have taken in Birmingham is untimely. Some have asked: "Why didn't you give the new city admini-stration time to act?" The only answer that I can give to this query is that the new Birmingham administration must be prodded about as much as the outgoing one, before it will act. We are sadly mistaken if we feel that the election of Albert Boutwell as mayor will bring the millennium to Birmingham.

While Mr. Boutwell is a much more gentle person than Mr. Connor, they are both segregationists, dedicated to maintenance of the status quo. I have hope that Mr. Boutwell will be reasonable enough to see the futility of massive resistance to desegregation. But he will not see this without pressure from devotees of civil rights. My friends, I must say to you that we have not made a single gain in civil rights without determined legal and nonviolent pressure. Lamentably, it is an historical fact that privileged groups seldom give up their privileges voluntarily. Individuals may see the moral light and voluntarily give up their unjust posture; but, as Reinhold Niebuhr has reminded us, groups tend to be more immoral than individuals.

We know through painful experience that freedom is never voluntarily given by the oppressor; it must be demanded by the oppressed. Frankly, I have yet to engage in a direct-action campaign that was "well timed" in the view of those who have not suffered unduly from the disease of segregation. For years now I have heard the word "Wait!" It rings in the ear of every Negro with piercing familiarity. This "Wait" has almost always meant 'Never." We must come to see, with one of our distinguished jurists, that "justice too long delayed is justice denied."

We have waited for more than 340 years for our constitutional and God-given rights. The nations of Asia and Africa are moving with jetlike speed toward gaining political independence, but we stiff creep at horse-and-buggy pace toward gaining a cup of coffee at a lunch counter. Perhaps it is easy for those who have never felt the stinging darts of segregation to say, "Wait." But when you have seen vicious mobs lynch your mothers and fathers at will and drown your sisters and brothers at whim; when you have seen hate-filled policemen curse, kick and even kill your black brothers and sisters; when you see the vast majority of your twenty million Negro brothers smothering in an airtight cage of poverty in the midst of an affluent society; when you suddenly find your tongue twisted and your speech stammering as you seek to explain to your six-year-old daughter why she can't go to the public amusement park that has just been advertised on television, and see tears welling up in her eyes when she is told that Funtown is closed to colored children, and see ominous clouds of inferiority beginning to form in her little mental sky, and see her beginning to distort her personality by developing an unconscious bitterness toward white people; when you have to concoct an answer for a five-year-old son who is asking: "Daddy, why do white people treat colored people so mean?"; when you take a cross-county drive and find it necessary to sleep night after night in the uncomfortable corners of your automobile because no motel will accept you; when you are humiliated day in and day out by nagging signs reading "white" and "colored"; when your first name becomes "nigger," your middle name becomes "boy" (however old you are) and your last name becomes "John," and your wife and mother are never given the respected title "Mrs."; when you are harried by day and haunted by night by the fact that you are a Negro, living constantly at tiptoe stance, never quite knowing what to expect next, and are plagued with inner fears and outer resentments; when you are forever fighting a degenerating sense of "nobodiness" then you will understand why we find it difficult to wait. There comes a time when the cup of endurance runs over, and men are no longer willing to be plunged into the abyss of despair. I hope, sirs, you can understand our legitimate and unavoidable impatience.

You express a great deal of anxiety over our willingness to break laws. This is certainly a legitimate concern. Since we so diligently urge people to obey the Supreme Court's decision of 1954 outlawing segregation in the public schools, at first glance it may seem rather paradoxical for us consciously to break laws. One may well ask: "How can you advocate breaking some laws and obeying others?" The answer lies in the fact that there fire two types of laws: just and unjust. I would be the Brat to advocate obeying just laws. One has not only a legal but a moral responsibility to obey just laws. Conversely, one has a moral responsibility to disobey unjust laws. I would agree with St. Augustine that "an unjust law is no law at all"

Now, what is the difference between the two? How does one determine whether a law is just or unjust? A just law is a man-made code that squares with the moral law or the law of God. An unjust law is a code that is out of harmony with the moral law. To put it in the terms of St. Thomas Aquinas: An unjust law is a human law that is not rooted in eternal law and natural law. Any law that uplifts human personality is just. Any law that degrades human personality is unjust. All segregation statutes are unjust because segregation distorts the soul and damages the personality. It gives the segregator a false sense of superiority and the segregated a false sense of inferiority. Segregation, to use the terminology of the Jewish philosopher Martin Buber, substitutes an "I-it" relationship for an "I-thou" relationship and ends up relegating persons to the status of things. Hence segregation is not only politically, economically and sociologically unsound, it is morally wrong and awful. Paul Tillich said that sin is separation. Is not segregation an existential expression 'of man's tragic separation, his awful estrangement, his terrible sinfulness? Thus it is that I can urge men to obey the 1954 decision of the Supreme Court, for it is morally right; and I can urge them to disobey segregation ordinances, for they are morally wrong.

Let us consider a more concrete example of just and unjust laws. An unjust law is a code that a numerical or power majority group compels a minority group to obey but does not make binding on itself. This is difference made legal. By the same token, a just law is a code that a majority compels a minority to follow and that it is willing to follow itself. This is sameness made legal.

Let me give another explanation. A law is unjust if it is inflicted on a minority that, as a result of being denied the right to vote, had no part in enacting or devising the law. Who can say that the legislature of Alabama which set up that state's segregation laws was democratically elected? Throughout Alabama all sorts of devious methods are used to prevent Negroes from becoming registered voters, and there are some counties in which, even though Negroes constitute a majority of the population, not a single Negro is registered. Can any law enacted under such circumstances be considered democratically structured?

Sometimes a law is just on its face and unjust in its application. For instance, I have been arrested on a charge of parading without a permit. Now, there is nothing wrong in having an ordinance which requires a permit for a parade. But such an ordinance becomes unjust when it is used to maintain segregation and to deny citizens the First Amendment privilege of peaceful assembly and protest.

I hope you are able to ace the distinction I am trying to point out. In no sense do I advocate evading or defying the law, as would the rabid segregationist. That would lead to anarchy. One who breaks an unjust law must do so openly, lovingly, and with a willingness to accept the penalty. I submit that an individual who breaks a law that conscience tells him is unjust and who willingly accepts the penalty of imprisonment in order to arouse the conscience of the community over its injustice, is in reality expressing the highest respect for law.

Of course, there is nothing new about this kind of civil disobedience. It was evidenced sublimely in the refusal of Shadrach, Meshach and Abednego to obey the laws of Nebuchadnezzar, on the ground that a higher moral law was at stake. It was practiced superbly by the early Christians, who were willing to face hungry lions and the excruciating pain of chopping blocks rather than submit to certain unjust laws of the Roman Empire. To a degree, academic freedom is a reality today because Socrates practiced civil disobedience. In our own nation, the Boston Tea Party represented a massive act of civil disobedience.

We should never forget that everything Adolf Hitler did in Germany was "legal" and everything the Hungarian freedom fighters did in Hungary was "illegal." It was "illegal" to aid and comfort a Jew in Hitler's Germany. Even so, I am sure that, had I lived in Germany at the time, I would have aided and comforted my Jewish brothers. If today I lived in a Communist country where certain principles dear to the Christian faith are suppressed, I would openly advocate disobeying that country's antireligious laws.

I must make two honest confessions to you, my Christian and Jewish brothers. First, I must confess that over the past few years I have been gravely disappointed with the white moderate. I have almost reached the regrettable conclusion that the Negro's great stumbling block in his stride toward freedom is not the White Citizen's Counciler or the Ku Klux Klanner, but the white moderate, who is more devoted to "order" than to justice; who prefers a negative peace which is the absence of tension to a positive peace which is the presence of justice; who constantly says: "I agree with you in the goal you seek, but I cannot agree with your methods of direct action"; who paternalistically believes he can set the timetable for another man's freedom; who lives by a mythical concept of time and who constantly advises the Negro to wait for a "more convenient season." Shallow understanding from people of good will is more frustrating than absolute misunderstanding from people of ill will. Lukewarm acceptance is much more bewildering than outright rejection.

I had hoped that the white moderate would understand that law and order exist for the purpose of establishing justice and that when they fail in this purpose they become the dangerously structured dams that block the flow of social progress. I had hoped that the white moderate would understand that the present tension in the South is a necessary phase of the transition from an obnoxious negative peace, in which the Negro passively accepted his unjust plight, to a substantive and positive peace, in which all men will respect the dignity and worth of human personality. Actually, we who engage in nonviolent direct action are not the creators of tension. We merely bring to the surface the hidden tension that is already alive. We bring it out in the open, where it can be seen and dealt with. Like a boil that can never be cured so long as it is covered up but must be opened with all its ugliness to the natural medicines of air and light, injustice must be exposed, with all the tension its exposure creates, to the light of human conscience and the air of national opinion before it can be cured.

In your statement you assert that our actions, even though peaceful, must be condemned because they precipitate violence. But is this a logical assertion? Isn't this like condemning a robbed man because his possession of money precipitated the evil act of robbery? Isn't this like condemning Socrates because his unswerving commitment to truth and his philosophical inquiries precipitated the act by the misguided populace in which they made him drink hemlock? Isn't this like condemning Jesus because his unique God-consciousness and never-ceasing devotion to God's will precipitated the evil act of crucifixion? We must come to see that, as the federal courts have consistently affirmed, it is wrong to urge an individual to cease his efforts to gain his basic constitutional rights because the quest may precipitate violence. Society must protect the robbed and punish the robber.

I had also hoped that the white moderate would reject the myth concerning time in relation to the struggle for freedom. I have just received a letter from a white brother in Texas. He writes: "And Christians know that the colored people will receive equal rights eventually, but it is possible that you are in too great a religious hurry. It has taken Christianity almost two thousand years to accomplish what it has. The teachings of Christ take time to come to earth." Such an attitude stems from a tragic misconception of time, from the strangely rational notion that there is something in the very flow of time that will inevitably cure all ills. Actually, time itself is neutral; it can be used either destructively or constructively. More and more I feel that the people of ill will have used time much more effectively than have the people of good will. We will have to repent in this generation not merely for the hateful words and actions of the bad people but for the appalling silence of the good people. Human progress never rolls in on wheels of inevitability; it comes through the tireless efforts of men willing to be co-workers with God, and without this 'hard work, time itself becomes an ally of the forces of social stagnation. We must use time creatively, in the knowledge that the time is always ripe to do right. Now is the time to make real the promise of democracy and transform our pending national elegy into a creative psalm of brotherhood. Now is the time to lift our national policy from the quicksand of racial injustice to the solid rock of human dignity.

You speak of our activity in Birmingham as extreme. At first I was rather disappointed that fellow clergymen would see my nonviolent efforts as those of an extremist. I began thinking about the fact that I stand in the middle of two opposing forces in the Negro community. One is a force of complacency, made up in part of Negroes who, as a result of long years of oppression, are so drained of self-respect and a sense of "somebodiness" that they have adjusted to segregation; and in part of a few middle class Negroes who, because of a degree of academic and economic security and because in some ways they profit by segregation, have become insensitive to the problems of the masses. The other force is one of bitterness and hatred, and it comes perilously close to advocating violence. It is expressed in the various black nationalist groups that are springing up across the nation, the largest and best-known being Elijah Muhammad's Muslim movement. Nourished by the Negro's frustration over the continued existence of racial discrimination, this movement is made up of people who have lost faith in America, who have absolutely repudiated Christianity, and who have concluded that the white man is an incorrigible "devil."

I have tried to stand between these two forces, saying that we need emulate neither the "do-nothingism" of the complacent nor the hatred and despair of the black nationalist. For there is the more excellent way of love and nonviolent protest. I am grateful to God that, through the influence of the Negro church, the way of nonviolence became an integral part of our struggle.

If this philosophy had not emerged, by now many streets of the South would, I am convinced, be flowing with blood. And I am further convinced that if our white brothers dismiss as "rabble-rousers" and "outside agitators" those of us who employ nonviolent direct action, and if they refuse to support our nonviolent efforts, millions of Negroes will, out of frustration and despair, seek solace and security in black-nationalist ideologies a development that would inevitably lead to a frightening racial nightmare.

Oppressed people cannot remain oppressed forever. The yearning for freedom eventually manifests itself, and that is what has happened to the American Negro. Something within has reminded him of his birthright of freedom, and something without has reminded him that it can be gained. Consciously or unconsciously, he has been caught up by the Zeitgeist, and with his black brothers of Africa and his brown and yellow brothers of Asia, South America and the Caribbean, the United States Negro is moving with a sense of great urgency toward the promised land of racial justice. If one recognizes this vital urge that has engulfed the Negro community, one should readily understand why public demonstrations are taking place. The Negro has many pent-up resentments and latent frustrations, and he must release them. So let him march; let him make prayer pilgrimages to the city hall; let him go on freedom rides-and try to understand why he must do so. If his repressed emotions are not released in nonviolent ways, they will seek expression through violence; this is not a threat but a fact of history. So I have not said to my people: "Get rid of your discontent." Rather, I have tried to say that this normal and healthy discontent can be channeled into the creative outlet of nonviolent direct action. And now this approach is being termed extremist.

But though I was initially disappointed at being categorized as an extremist, as I continued to think about the matter I gradually gained a measure of satisfaction from the label. Was not Jesus an extremist for love: "Love your enemies, bless them that curse you, do good to them that hate you, and pray for them which despitefully use you, and persecute you." Was not Amos an extremist for justice: "Let justice roll down like waters and righteousness like an ever-flowing stream." Was not Paul an extremist for the Christian gospel: "I bear in my body the marks of the Lord Jesus." Was not Martin Luther an extremist:

"Here I stand; I cannot do otherwise, so help me God." And John Bunyan: "I will stay in jail to the end of my days before I make a butchery of my conscience." And Abraham Lincoln: "This nation cannot survive half slave and half free." And Thomas Jefferson: "We hold these truths to be self-evident, that all men are created equal ..." So the question is not whether we will be extremists, but what kind of extremists we will be. Will we be extremists for hate or for love? Will we be extremists for the preservation of injustice or for the extension of justice? In that dramatic scene on Calvary's hill three men were crucified. We must never forget that all three were crucified for the same crime—the crime of extremism. Two were extremists for immorality, and thus fell below their environment. The other, Jesus Christ, was an extremist for love, truth and goodness, and thereby rose above his environment. Perhaps the South, the nation and the world are in dire need of creative extremists.

I had hoped that the white moderate would see this need. Perhaps I was too optimistic; perhaps I expected too much. I suppose I should have realized that few members of the oppressor race can understand the deep groans and passionate yearnings of the oppressed race, and still fewer have the vision to see that injustice must be rooted out by strong, persistent and determined action. I am thankful, however, that some of our white brothers in the South have grasped the meaning of this social revolution and committed themselves to it. They are still too few in quantity, but they are big in quality. Some-such as Ralph McGill, Lillian Smith, Harry Golden, James McBride Dabbs, Ann Braden and Sarah Patton Boyle—have written about our struggle in eloquent and prophetic terms. Others have marched with us down nameless streets of the South. They have languished in filthy, roach-infested jails, suffering the abuse and brutality of policemen who view them as "dirty nigger lovers." Unlike so many of their moderate brothers and sisters, they have recognized the urgency of the moment and sensed the need for powerful "action" antidotes to combat the disease of segregation.

Let me take note of my other major disappointment. I have been so greatly disappointed with the white church and its leadership. Of course, there are some notable exceptions. I am not unmindful of the fact that each of you has taken some significant stands on this issue. I commend you, Reverend Stallings, for your Christian stand on this past Sunday, in welcoming Negroes to your worship service on a non segregated basis. I commend the Catholic leaders of this state for integrating Spring Hill College several years ago.

But despite these notable exceptions, I must honestly reiterate that I have been disappointed with the church. I do not say this as one of those negative critics who can always find something wrong with the church. I say this as a minister of the gospel, who loves the church; who was nurtured in its bosom; who 'has been sustained by its spiritual blessings and who will remain true to it as long as the cord of Rio shall lengthen.

When I was suddenly catapulted into the leadership of the bus protest in Montgomery, Alabama, a few years ago, I felt we would be supported by the white church; felt that the white ministers, priests and rabbis of the South would be among our strongest allies. Instead, some have been outright opponents, refusing to understand the freedom movement and misrepresenting its leader era; and too many others have been more cautious than courageous and have remained silent behind the anesthetizing security of stained-glass windows.

In spite of my shattered dreams, I came to Birmingham with the hope that the white religious leadership of this community would see the justice of our cause and, with deep moral concern, would serve as the channel through which our just grievances could reach the power structure. I had hoped that each of you would understand. But again I have been disappointed.

I have heard numerous southern religious leaders admonish their worshipers to comply with a desegregation decision because it is the law, but I have longed to hear white ministers declare: "Follow this decree because integration is morally right and because the Negro is your brother." In the midst of blatant injustices inflicted upon the Negro, I have watched white churchmen stand on the sideline and mouth pious irrelevancies and sanctimonious trivialities. In the midst of a mighty struggle to rid our nation of racial and economic injustice, I have heard many ministers say: "Those are social issues, with which the gospel has no real concern." And I have watched many churches commit themselves to a completely other worldly religion which makes a strange, un-Biblical distinction between body and soul, between the sacred and the secular.

I have traveled the length and breadth of Alabama, Mississippi and all the other southern states. On sweltering summer days and crisp autumn mornings I have looked at the South's beautiful churches with their lofty spires pointing heavenward. I have beheld the impressive outlines of her massive religious-education buildings. Over and over I have found myself asking: "What kind of people worship here? Who is their God? Where were their voices when the lips of Governor Barnett dripped with words of interposition and nullification? Where were they when Governor Walleye gave a clarion call for defiance and hatred? Where were their voices of support when bruised and weary Negro men and women decided to rise from the dark dungeons of complacency to the bright hills of creative protest?"

Yes, these questions are still in my mind. In deep disappointment I have wept over the laxity of the church. But be assured that my tears have been tears of love. There can be no deep disappointment where there is not deep love. Yes, I love the church. How could I do otherwise? I am in the rather unique position of being the son, the grandson and the great-grandson of preachers. Yes, I see the church as the body of Christ. But, oh! How we have blemished and scarred that body through social neglect and through fear of being nonconformists.

There was a time when the church was very powerful in the time when the early Christians rejoiced at being deemed worthy to suffer for what they believed. In those days the church was not merely a thermometer that recorded the ideas and principles of popular opinion; it was a thermostat that transformed the mores of society. Whenever the early Christians entered a town, the people in power became disturbed and immediately sought to convict the Christians for being "disturbers of the peace" and "outside agitators"' But the Christians pressed on, in the conviction that they were "a colony of heaven," called to obey God rather than man. Small in number, they were big in commitment. They were too God intoxicated to be "astronomically intimidated." By their effort and example they brought an end to such ancient evils as infanticide and gladiatorial contests.

Things are different now. So often the contemporary church is a weak, ineffectual voice with an uncertain sound. So often it is an archdefender of the status quo. Far from being disturbed by the presence of the church, the power structure of the average community is consoled by the church's silent and often even vocal sanction of things as they are.

But the judgment of God is upon the church as never before. If today's church does not recapture the sacrificial spirit of the early church, it will lose its authenticity, forfeit the loyalty of millions, and be dismissed as an irrelevant social club with no meaning for the twentieth century. Every day I meet young people whose disappointment with the church has turned into outright disgust.

Perhaps I have once again been too optimistic. Is organized religion too inextricably bound to the status quo to save our nation and the world? Perhaps I must turn my faith to the inner spiritual church, the church within the church, as the true *ekklesia* and the hope of the world. But again I am thankful to God that some noble souls from the ranks of organized religion have broken loose from the paralyzing chains of conformity and joined us as active partners in the struggle for freedom, They have left their secure congregations and walked the streets of Albany, Georgia, with us. They have gone down the highways of the South on tortuous rides for freedom. Yes, they have gone to jail with us. Some have been dismissed from their churches, have lost the support of their bishops and fellow ministers. But they have acted in the faith that right defeated is stronger than evil triumphant. Their witness has been the spiritual salt that has preserved the true meaning of the gospel in these troubled times. They have carved a tunnel of hope through the dark mountain of disappointment.

I hope the church as a whole will meet the challenge of this decisive hour. But even if the church does not come to the aid of justice, I have no despair about the future. I have no fear about the outcome of our struggle in Birmingham, even if our motives are at present misunderstood. We will reach the goal of freedom in Birmingham and all over the nation, because the goal of America is freedom. Abused and scorned though we may be, our destiny is tied up with America's destiny. Before the pilgrims landed at Plymouth, we were here. Before the pen of Jefferson etched the majestic words of the Declaration of Independence across the pages of history, we were here. For more than two centuries our forebears labored in this country without wages; they made cotton king; they built the homes of their masters while suffering gross injustice and shameful humiliation-and yet out of a bottomless vitality they continued to thrive and develop. If the inexpressible cruelties of slavery could not stop us, the opposition we now face will surely fail. We will win our freedom because the sacred heritage of our nation and the eternal will of God are embodied in our echoing demands.

Before closing I feel impelled to mention one other point in your statement that has troubled me profoundly. You warmly commended the Birmingham police force for keeping "order" and "preventing violence." I doubt that you would have so warmly commended the police force if you had seen its dogs sinking their teeth into unarmed, nonviolent Negroes. I doubt that you would so quickly commend the policemen if .you were to observe their ugly and inhumane treatment of Negroes here in the city jail; if you were to watch them push and curse old Negro women and young Negro girls; if you were to see them slap and kick old Negro men and young boys; if you were to observe them, as they did on two occasions, refuse to give us food because we wanted to sing our grace together. I cannot join you in your praise of the Birmingham police department.

It is true that the police have exercised a degree of discipline in handing the demonstrators. In this sense they have conducted themselves rather "nonviolently" in public. But for what purpose? To preserve the evil system of segregation. Over the past few years I have consistently preached that nonviolence demands that the means we use must be as pure as the ends we seek. I have tried to make clear that it is wrong to use immoral means to attain moral ends. But now I must affirm that it is just as wrong, or perhaps even more so, to use moral means to preserve immoral ends. Perhaps Mr. Connor and his policemen have been rather nonviolent in public, as was Chief Pritchett in Albany, Georgia but they have used the moral means of nonviolence to maintain the immoral end of racial injustice. As T. S. Eliot has said: "The last temptation is the greatest treason: To do the right deed for the wrong reason."

I wish you had commended the Negro sit-inners and demonstrators of Birmingham for their sublime courage, their willingness to suffer and their amazing discipline in the midst of great provocation. One day the South will recognize its real heroes. They will be the James Merediths, with the noble sense of purpose that enables them to face jeering and hostile mobs, and with the agonizing loneliness that characterizes the life of the pioneer. They will be old, oppressed, battered Negro women, symbolized in a seventy-two-year-old woman in Montgomery, Alabama, who rose up with a sense of dignity and with her people decided not to ride segregated buses, and who responded with ungrammatical profundity to one who inquired about her weariness: "My feets is tired, but my soul is at rest." They will be the young high school and college students, the young ministers of the gospel and a host of their elders, courageously and nonviolently sitting in at lunch counters and willingly going to jail for conscience' sake. One day the South will know that when these disinherited children of God sat down at lunch counters, they were in reality standing up for what is best in the American dream and for the most sacred values in our Judeo-Christian heritage, thereby bringing our nation back to those great wells of democracy which were dug deep by the founding fathers in their formulation of the Constitution and the Declaration of Independence.

Never before have I written so long a letter. I'm afraid it is much too long to take your precious time. I can assure you that it would have been much shorter if I had been writing from a comfortable desk, but what else can one do when he is alone in a narrow jail cell, other than write long letters, think long thoughts and pray long prayers?

If I have said anything in this letter that overstates the truth and indicates an unreasonable impatience, I beg you to forgive me. If I have said anything that understates the truth and indicates my having a patience that allows me to settle for anything less than brotherhood, I beg God to forgive me.

I hope this letter finds you strong in the faith. I also hope that circumstances will soon make it possible for me to meet each of you, not as an integrationist or a civil rights leader but as a fellow clergyman and a Christian brother. Let us all hope that the dark clouds of racial prejudice will soon pass away and the deep fog of misunderstanding will be lifted from our fear-drenched communities, and in some not too distant tomorrow the radiant stars of love and brotherhood will shine over our great nation with all their scintillating beauty.

APPENDIX C
ABRAHAM LINCOLN'S SECOND
INAUGURAL ADDRESS

March 4, 1865

At this second appearing to take the oath of the presidential office, there is less occasion for an extended address than there was at the first. Then a statement, somewhat in detail, of a course to be pursued, seemed fitting and proper. Now, at the expiration of four years, during which public declarations have been constantly called forth on every point and phase of the great contest which still absorbs the attention, and engrosses the energies of the nation, little that is new could be presented. The progress of our arms, upon which all else chiefly depends, is as well known to the public as to myself; and it is, I trust, reasonably satisfactory and encouraging to all. With high hope for the future, no prediction in regard to it is ventured.

On the occasion corresponding to this four years ago, all thoughts were anxiously directed to an impending civil war. All dreaded it—all sought to avert it. While the inaugeral [sic] address was being delivered from this place, devoted altogether to saving the Union without war, insurgent agents were in the city seeking to destroy it without war—seeking to dissole [sic] the Union, and divide effects, by negotiation. Both parties deprecated war; but one of them would make war rather than let the nation survive; and the other would accept war rather than let it perish. And the war came.

One eighth of the whole population were colored slaves, not distributed generally over the Union, but localized in the Southern part of it. These slaves constituted a peculiar and powerful interest. All knew that this interest was, somehow, the cause of the war. To strengthen, perpetuate, and extend this interest was the object for which the insurgents would rend the Union, even by war; while the government claimed no right to do more than to restrict the territorial enlargement of it. Neither party expected for the war, the magnitude, or the duration, which it has already attained. Neither anticipated that the cause of the conflict might cease with, or even before, the conflict itself should cease. Each looked for an easier triumph, and a result less fundamental and astounding. Both read the same Bible, and pray to the same God; and each invokes His aid against the other. It may seem strange that any men should dare to ask a just God's assistance in wringing their bread from the sweat of other men's faces; but let us judge not that we be not judged. The prayers of both could not be answered; that of neither has been answered fully. The Almighty has his own purposes. "Woe unto the world because of offences! for it must needs be that offences come; but woe to that man by whom the offence cometh!" If we shall suppose that American Slavery is one of those offences which, in the providence of God, must needs come, but which, having continued through His appointed time, He now wills to remove, and that He gives to both North and South, this terrible war, as the woe due to those by whom the offence came, shall we discern therein any departure from those divine attributes which the believers in a Living God always ascribe to Him? Fondly do we hope—fervently do we pray—that this mighty scourge of war may speedily pass away. Yet, if God wills that it continue, until all the wealth piled by the bond-man's two hundred and fifty years of unrequited toil shall be sunk, and until every drop of blood drawn with the lash, shall be paid by another drawn with the sword, as was said three thousand years ago, so still it must be said "the judgments of the Lord, are true and righteous altogether."

With malice toward none; with charity for all; with firmness in the right, as God gives us to see the right, let us strive on to finish the work we are in; to bind up the nation's wounds; to care for him who shall have borne the battle, and for his widow, and his orphan—to do all which may achieve and cherish a just and lasting peace, among ourselves, and with all nations.

APPENDIX D
THOMAS JEFFERSON'S LETTER TO THE DANBURY BAPTISTS

January 1, 1802

Gentlemen:

The affectionate sentiments of esteem and approbation which you are so good as to express towards me, on behalf of the Danbury Baptist association, give me the highest satisfaction. my duties dictate a faithful and zealous pursuit of the interests of my constituents, & in proportion as they are persuaded of my fidelity to those duties, the discharge of them becomes more and more pleasing.

Believing with you that religion is a matter which lies solely between Man & his God, that he owes account to none other for his faith or his worship, that the legitimate powers of government reach actions only, & not opinions, I contemplate with sovereign reverence that act of the whole American people which declared that their legislature should "make no law respecting an establishment of religion, or prohibiting the free exercise thereof," thus building a wall of separation between Church & State. Adhering to this expression of the supreme will of the nation in behalf of the rights of conscience, I shall see with sincere satisfaction the progress of those sentiments which tend to restore to man all his natural rights, convinced he has no natural right in opposition to his social duties.

I reciprocate your kind prayers for the protection & blessing of the common father and creator of man, and tender you for yourselves & your religious association, assurances of my high respect & esteem.

APPENDIX E
EISENHOWER'S IN CASE OF FAILURE DRAFT STATEMENT CONCERNING D-DAY

June 5, 1944

[Note to reader: In the original document located at the Dwight D. Eisenhower Presidential Library in Abilene, Kansas, Eisenhower made the mistake of dating it as July instead of June.]

Our landings in the Cherbourg-Havre area have failed to gain a satisfactory foothold and I have withdrawn the troops. My decision to attack at this time and place was based upon the best information available. The troops, the Air and the Navy did all that bravery and devotion could do. If any blame or fault attaches to the attempt it is mine alone.

APPENDIX F
EXCERPT FROM DR. NOVELLO'S COMMENCEMENT SPEECH AT PROVIDENCE COLLEGE

May 17, 1992

So what better than to invite the first woman Surgeon General of this land to share some thoughts with you on your graduation day--my office is like your University, small but powerful in messages and responsibilities.

Since becoming Surgeon General I have traveled to many cities and countries, and I have met many people. I have met the brightest and the most fortunate—and I have met many others who are less fortunate and lack even the most basic of necessities.

But the one key fact that continues to ring true is that each one of us in spite of the odds, has a most wonderful opportunity to make a difference. As new college graduates, that point is especially true for you today.

Whether or not each one of you will reach the pinnacle of success in your personal path or professional lives, is a relative matter, shaped by internal and external influences throughout your lives, and the goals that you have set for yourselves. Setting your goals is extremely important. After all, if you don't know where you're going, you're already there.

Set your goals high, but plan realistically and thoughtfully. Dare to reach for the stars, but remember that while getting there is important, how you get there matters most. Remember that even failure can be a useful experience, because there are things you will learn along the way that will shape your life.

That is why it is such a joy for me to join you today in celebrating this outstanding institution and to share your pride in these fine young men and women who will now carry your legacy into the future....

Today marks both an end and a beginning for you. It is the end of your student life—a time when your efforts and responsibilities were wholly concentrated on your studies. It is also the beginning of your life as an educated, responsible adult citizen.

A beginning. Your education, like life itself, is a journey, not a destination.

Many of you will proceed to advanced education. Some of you will continue your education outside of an academic setting. You have been well prepared to tackle anything by this College and its distinguished faculty.

Your parents, instructors, and peers have helped to shape your aspirations, and this wonderful institution has provided you with the means to get there. However, let me say to you, do not get overly comfortable or complacent in your position.

Think about it. After four years of all-night cramming for exams, much of what you've learned will soon be obsolete. Have no fear. You have learned to learn. You can and must continue to do so.

It troubles me that so much of higher education must be spent in the drudgery of memorizing facts and dates—and so little time spent on such things that would fall under the umbrella of pure common sense.

Now, facts are necessary. They are the building blocks of our knowledge. Without them, judgment is impossible, honesty is irrelevant, and compassion is fraudulent...but facts change.

Consider that five years from today, most of the science and technology you have learned so far will have changed dramatically. Even worse, in ten years you probably won't remember more than 10 percent of all the facts you have had crammed into your heads. So start practicing a healthy skepticism, because so much of what you have been taught, while accurate or accepted now, may not stand the test of time.

So then, what is the true purpose of your education? Not the accumulation of facts that have been given to you. Something much more precious: A habit of mind, a philosophy of life, a way of being.

Cherish this gift. It is what will set you apart, give you dignity, and make your life precious not only to you but to the others you meet. It is important that you continue to question, to challenge ideas, to test new ones, for this is truly how we learn and how life advances.

Socrates said that if he was wiser than all the rest of Ancient Greece, it was only because he knew what he didn't know.

That is why I prefer to evaluate people not so much on the answers they give, but on the questions they ask.

Dear graduates, the decades ahead will be filled with societal and technological changes that will challenge the best among you. And for some of the challenges you will not be prepared. In fact, none of us here will be prepared.

No matter what career path you choose, you will be at the center of ever more complex questions. Dealing with such questions will require that you maintain your curiosity and continue to study arts, science and technology, balanced by a lifelong interest in the humanities and compassion for our fellow human beings.

As I said before, you are embarking on a journey that literally has no destination—except that you do your very best on behalf of your society and your fellow man.

DISCUSSION GUIDE

CHAPTER ONE

1. Why are there still places in the world where different lives are treated differently? For example, prior to the U.S. intervention in Afghanistan, men and women were given different rights. Why do you think this happened?

2. Dr. King refused to blame the founders of our nation for failing to include African Americans. Yet he believed that the "great wells of democracy" that were "dug deep by the Founding Fathers" could be used by each new generation to expand the circle of freedom to more people. What are some examples of this?

3. What are some examples in your own life of how your country values you?

ASSIGNMENT: Volunteer at a retirement center or a hospital and help others feel that they are special through your service. This can be your own way to show how your country honors all its citizens.

CHAPTER TWO

1. Why are families so important to our society?

2. Why are families necessary to have a "virtuous republic"?

3. What are some things you want to do (or not do) when you become a parent?

ASSIGNMENT: Sit down for an interview with one of your parents. Ask him/her about being a parent. What's the hardest part? The best part? The most rewarding part? Write a one-page summary of your interview and talk about what you've learned about families.

CHAPTER THREE

1. Why was the sight of George Washington wearing a pair of glasses such a revelation to his officers?

2. Why are great leaders almost always associated with great causes?

3. Is helping others the best way to help yourself? Why?

ASSIGNMENT: Find a local charity and commit yourself to giving your time and effort to this cause over the course of the next year. See if it doesn't make a difference in how you view others and yourself.

CHAPTER FOUR

1. Why did the Signer of the Declaration risk everything for their cause?

2. When was the last time you took a risk? What did you risk?

3. In a free society, why is it important to serve others?

4. What are some ways you can serve others?

ASSIGNMENT: Spend ten hours this month volunteering at a soup kitchen or a nursing home.

CHAPTER FIVE

1. Why did Dr. King try and convert, rather than conquer, his enemies?

2. What did equality mean to the Founding Fathers?

3. What are some ways you can be prepared for your future?

ASSIGNMENT: Try and spend some time with a person at school you don't know very well. Find out about him/her. What are his/her goals? Is there any way you can use your "virtue and talents" to help him/her achieve those goals?

CHAPTER SIX

1. Why did Rosa Parks refuse to move from her seat on the bus? What gave her the courage to stand her ground?

2. Where is the real power of justice found in America: in our courts or in our people? Why?

3. What are some examples of how ordinary Americans helped promote justice?

ASSIGNMENT: Find a church or a community center that is reaching out with social justice programs to the community you live in. Volunteer your time with that organization.

CHAPTER SEVEN

1. Why did Lincoln have so much compassion for the South?

2. What did he hope to accomplish by promoting compassionate policies toward the South?

3. What are some ways you can show compassion in your community?

ASSIGNMENT: Identify three people in your life who are less fortunate than you. Map out a plan of things you can do to help ease their burden. Then start doing it.

CHAPTER EIGHT

1. What did Thomas Jefferson mean by a "wall" that would separate church and state?

2. What does the First Amendment say about the establishment of a national church?

3. Martin Luther King, Jr., is an example of a man of faith entering the public square and making a difference. Can you think of others?

ASSIGNMENT: Read Jefferson's complete letter to the Danbury Baptist Association. Think of a list of ways you can use your faith to help improve society.

CHAPTER NINE

1. Why did Eisenhower feel it was his responsibility to accept the blame if D-Day failed?

2. What are some of the excuses you have heard people use to blame others when things go wrong?

3. Why do only half of registered voters vote in elections?

ASSIGNMENT: If you are eighteen, go to the county courthouse, fill out the paperwork, and register to vote. Or, perhaps more important, go and register someone else to vote.

CHAPTER TEN

1. Why did NASA spawn so many new inventions?

2. Why was the space race a product of the Cold War?

3. What did Armstrong mean he said landing on the moon was a "giant leap for mankind."

ASSIGNMENT: Write out a goal for yourself. Be specific. Have a schedule. And map out a plan for achieving it.

CHAPTER ELEVEN

1. How did FDR's polio change him personally?

2. What did Frost mean when he spoke of his choice of the road less traveled making "all the difference"?

3. Why do so many people go with the flow rather than doing what is right?

ASSIGNMENT: Make a friend with someone outside of your social crowd at school.

CHAPTER TWELVE

1. Have you had any unique experiences in life that give you a special perspective?

2. How can you use those experiences to create your own unique vision for life?

3. What does it mean to put away your mirrors?

ASSIGNMENT: Write out a vision for your life, including how you intend to help others.